Outrageous

Women

Outrageous

God

WOMEN

IN THE

FIRST

TWO

GENERATIONS OF

CHRISTIANITY

Outrageous Women Outrageous God

WOMEN IN THE FIRST TWO GENERATIONS OF CHRISTIANITY

Ross Saunders

E J DWYER

First published in 1996 by
E. J. Dwyer (Australia) Pty Ltd
Unit 13, Perry Park
33 Maddox Street
Alexandria NSW 2015
Australia
Phone: (02) 550 2355
Fax: (02) 519 3218

National Library of Australia
Cataloguing-in-Publication data
Saunders, Ross 1926– .
Outrageous women, outrageous God: women in the first two generations of Christianity.

Bibliography.
Includes index.
ISBN 0 85574 278 X.

1. Women in Christianity – History – Early church, ca. 30–600. 2. Women in the Bible. 3. Woman (Christian theology) – History of doctrines – Early church, ca. 30–600.
I. Title.

261.834409015

Cover design by Mango Design Group Pty Ltd
Text design by NB Design
Typeset in 11.5pt/14pt Bembo by Post Typesetters, Brisbane
Printed in Australia by Griffin Paperbacks, Netley, S.A.

10 9 8 7 6 5 4 3 2 1
00 99 98 97 96

Distributed in the United States by:
    Morehouse Publishing
    871 Ethan Allen Highway
    RIDGEFIELD CT 06877
    Ph: (203) 431 3927
    Fax: (203) 431 3964

Distributed in Ireland and the U.K. by:
    Columba Book Service
    93 The Rise
    Mount Merrion
    BLACKROCK CO. DUBLIN
    Ph: (01) 283 2954
    Fax: (01) 288 3770

Contents

Preface

This book began in 1993 when the Community of the Sisters of the Church, an order of Anglican sisters at Glebe, (in Sydney, Australia), asked me to give a talk to their chapter meeting. I decided that, as they were a group of very positive and determined women, struggling to regain some of the momentum they had lost with the closure of their St Catherine's School, a fresh examination of the status and ministry of women in the New Testament and how even God approved of the way they went against many of the social and religious constraints of their time, would be useful to them.

The following year the sisters asked me to continue what I had begun and take this study into the early second century.

What follows is a fresh approach to the place women, both Jewish and gentile, made for themselves from the conception of John the Baptizer to the death of the last apostle.

When you stop to consider that all the authors of the New Testament books were men who themselves were part of the constraints that society and religion placed upon women, then you can't help being amazed at the extent to which women gained prominence in early Christianity.

I've used the word "outrageous" to describe these women and their actions to emphasize just how far some of them stepped outside what was traditionally allowed them in their own society. I do not mean to imply, of course, that they did anything sinful; but I do mean to say that they would have caused many a male and female eyebrow to be raised!

That God would not only allow such behavior but at times encourage it, means that to some extent God is the origin of this outrageousness.

May this book help those of you who are feeling the inner urge to go beyond the place in which both the church and society have confined you. May it encourage you by showing you that such urgings were there especially among women in the very first days of the church.

I dedicate this book to Sister Frances and her band of outrageous co-workers, and commit the royalties from its sale to their work.

Introduction

If you were asked to name an outrageous woman in the New Testament you would no doubt mention either Herodias or her daughter Salome.

Herodias had wiggled her Middle Eastern hips and flashed her black eyes much too often at her powerful brother-in-law, King Herod, resulting in his breaking the Jewish law and marrying her while her divorced husband Philip was still alive. And she maintained her grip on him when John the Baptizer exposed their misalliance, encouraging her daughter Salome to demand the Baptizer's head on a silver salver after provocatively dancing Herod into erotic powerlessness.

But I have in mind a much different kind of outrageousness. I mean being outrageous to the extent of breaking with man-made convention and demanding to be heard, seen, or to be allowed to carry out actions normally permitted only to men at times when men seem inhibited for some reason or other in taking up those responsibilities they had arrogated to themselves in the first place.

There is evidence all around us today of Australian Koori women leading their menfolk in recovering and preserving their indigenous culture, teaching their children bush craft and even becoming tribal elders—a phenomenon unheard of a thousand years ago—while their menfolk tend to dissipate their broken morale in drugs and grog.

Australia's first Koori magistrate is a woman. Australia's first recognized Koori poet is a woman. In so many spheres it is indigenous women who are taking up the gauntlet for their people.

The same phenomenon can be seen in many other indigenous groups around the world today: outrageous women are leading their people in the struggle for equality and human rights. Outrageous, because they dare to step outside the position society had constructed for them.

Because we are not as familiar as we should be with the place of women in the Mediterranean society of the New Testament period, we often fail to see the large number of outrageous women who feature in the life of the early church.

In part 1 of the book I will deal with those women who are named in the gospels, while in part 2 I will follow with those named in the book of Acts. In part 3 I will deal with those named in the epistles. In part 4 I will take a fresh look at how Paul constructed the place of women in the early congregations, and in part 5 I will show how women disappear almost entirely from the early post-apostolic church.

My sincere hope is those of you who are men will realize the need to give back to women their rightful place in the kingdom of God, and that those of you who are women and feel the tug of Holy Spirit in your innards will respond by offering yourselves wholeheartedly and optimistically for both lay and ordained ministry in Christ's church.

2

PART 1 | *Mediterranean Societies*

It's so easy to read about those people who lived in the first century of our era and then think that we can readily understand them by simply putting our own minds into their heads. We figure that people haven't changed all that much over the centuries. We just need to make allowances for language, technology and communications, and there they are: reflections of ourselves!

Sociologists have tried to make our task easier. Their studies of nineteenth- and twentieth-century communities have led them to devise models that help explain how people behave in given situations and societies. But when they tried to apply those models to older societies, they found that they didn't quite work. In the process of adapting and refining their models to account for older societies, they fell into the trap of reading their own mindset back into the ancient world, with the inevitable result that the ancients started to look and talk like us.

The same problem showed up when scholars began translating the classical writings: Plato began sounding like Descartes and Euripides like Shakespeare!

Anthropologists have long tried to study ancient societies and to understand them on their own terms. They have made honest efforts to analyze the way traditional societies have operated. Cultural anthropologists, in particular, have tried to include a broader perspective, searching for ways to enter the mindset of people of different centuries and with histories different to our own.

Putting some of these disciplines together, it is now more possible than ever before to eavesdrop, as it were, on people of earlier times whose histories took paths different to ours. We are the strangers—not they. We are the foreigners traveling back in time, standing on the outskirts of their villages and towns, walking up and down their marketplaces, listening in to their conversations and watching with awe their social rituals and ceremonies, struggling to understand them on their own terms, in their own words.

What I want to do is to outline those social aspects of the Mediterranean world that will help you to understand the place of women, and show how early Christianity went about trying to change some of the social relationships that seemed inappropriate for all those who chose to follow the Way of Jesus.

1. The Mediterranean Model

What the cultural anthropologists have discovered is that all those societies that lived around the Mediterranean Sea during the period of the Greek and Roman empires shared many cultural concepts. In spite of local language differences, the Greek language remained the lingua franca for many centuries, but especially during the first century of our era. Thus we can refer to these people as "typical Mediterraneans", whether they came from Greece, Italy, north Africa, Spain, Egypt, Israel, western Asia or the various islands in the Mediterranean, Ionian and Aegean seas.

Here, then, are four core values of these societies. And for each core value there were strategies—what the anthropologists call "means values"—for maintaining those core values.

Honor and Shame

"Honor" is a combination of your assessment of your place in the community plus the community's assessment of your place.

In the first-century Mediterranean world everyone belonged in a great procession: the most honored person at one end, the least honored at the other. Your place in that procession was determined almost exclusively by the status of your father and the status of your family and tribe. Each person was expected to act in ways appropriate to their status. Attempts to act in ways that were perceived to be aimed at moving your place in the procession more towards the head would cause you to be jeered at—even dishonored. No-one, of course, wanted to go further down the line!

But there were acceptable ways by which you could advance yourself. You could become an athlete, compete in games and win. This would result in your being attributed *arete*—excellence. While you kept on winning, your *arete* would guarantee you a place somewhat ahead of your natural place in the procession. But once you came second, then you lost all your *arete* and would be returned to your normal place.

If you were a man, then you could try and become a religious teacher—a scribe. But if you came from a place well down in the procession, you would need the patronage of someone near the head of the procession, making you permanently in that patron's debt.

If you were a peasant, and therefore near the bottom end of the procession, then you could train to become an artisan—a carpenter, stonemason, leatherworker, potter and so on. But trades such as these advanced you only one or two places up, since generally artisans were not accorded much honor at all. While artisans were in constant demand and their products valued, they themselves had lowly status. The

5

problem you would face here is that, if you happened to be the eldest son in the family, you were expected to follow in your father's trade or position. If your father happened to be a peasant share farmer and you decided to become a carpenter, the moment you left home to learn carpentry, your father and your family name would be dishonored. Also, you had no place of honor until your father died, when you would take over as family head and as maintainer of the family's place of honor in the procession.

It is worth remembering here that Jesus himself dishonored his dead father Joseph's name when he left home to begin his mission. He himself was thus the cause of offense to his home town, Nazareth. This explains the reaction of his fellow villagers when, after his baptism and testing in the wilderness, he returned to Nazareth and went to the synagogue where he had gone since he was a child. At first, they listened in awe to his words; but then they remembered how he had left home, dishonored his father's name and left his mother and unmarried sisters to fend for themselves instead of being their sponsor and carer.[1]

And when Jesus called his first disciples, there were several who were eldest sons. He called upon them to act in a way that was considered dishonorable when he insisted that they leave home and follow him.

It was not sufficient, however, just to be aware of your place in the status procession. You were expected to maintain your honor by acknowledging your community and making sure you kept that community in its place relative to neighboring communities.

If you happened to own your own land and house, then you were expected to make donations to your community institutions. In the case of the Jewish communities we are most interested in, this could involve endowing lectureships for scribes to come from Jerusalem and teach in your local synagogue; providing money for new furniture for your synagogue; paying for the replacement of a worn-out scroll of scripture; paying for a memorial to a famous religious leader, and so on.

In doing any of these things your name would be written up for all to see that you had fulfilled your duty of honor maintenance. The higher up your place in the procession, the more you would be expected to share with your community.

It is important here to understand that gifts of money to help the poor were not regarded as honor maintenance. While the community leaders were in a position to reciprocate by paying for your name to be inscribed in stone or wood, the poor would not be able to do so.

When the rich young ruler came to Jesus and asked what he should do to inherit eternal life, he was told to sell everything and give to the poor. Had this young man of high status done what Jesus commanded, he would have acted in two ways that would have brought him into dishonor in the eyes of his community. In the first place, having sold everything his father had left to him he would be in no position to carry out his honorable duties of making gifts to his community. In the second, giving everything away to the poor would have brought him more dishonor, as no-one regarded giving to the poor an honorable action. The poor were born that way and deserved only to stay in their poverty. The only ones in need that you helped were those of your own status who had lost their money because of a war or a bad investment. You did that because one day you might need them to reciprocate.

This young man could not face a life of being dishonored, and so he walked away sadly. It needs to be remembered that he was attached to his honor and not to his money and possessions: the money was what allowed him to maintain his honorable status in the eyes of himself and his community.

Another means of maintaining honor was to practice

7

hospitality. You would regularly entertain with dinners. You would invite to your dinner only those on the same social level as you. You would select your guest list carefully and make it public, so that those you had not invited would know. You would expect those you invited to invite you in turn to their home for dinner.

Dinners and feasts were a very important means of signaling your own social status and demonstrating that you accepted your responsibility of maintaining your honorable status in your community. You would never invite anyone of lower status than you to a dinner, for that would be to risk being dishonored. Nor would you invite anyone above you, for that would be interpreted to mean that you were pretending to be on a higher level than you actually were.

We should understand, then, that hospitality did not arise from any desire to help those in need nor to express friendship. When the New Testament exhorts christians to be hospitable, we must understand it to mean that sort of hospitality that was not based upon honor maintenance, but based upon the responsibility of sharing your blessings with others and meeting their needs, irrespective of their social standing in relation to yours.

Maintaining one's honorable position in the eyes of one's community was the single most powerful driving force in the whole of the first-century Mediterranean world.

Only males were accorded honor. Women were recognized only in relationship to some man: a father, an uncle, a grandfather, a brother, a husband, a son. They had no honor: they reflected the honor of the man who was their sponsor. But they had a sense of shame. Their primary role was to protect their sponsor's honor by behaving in a positive, virginal manner. They had to be careful that in public they dressed and behaved demurely, spoke to men only when spoken to, were seen only with men who had the same honor status as their sponsor's and that they were in circumstances that could not be misconstrued.

The physical virginity of a woman was important as it symbolized her sense of shame. Only her groom could break that barrier and thus claim her as his honorable partner. Women could not take part in sport of any kind, not only because Greek and Roman games expected nudity of the competitors, but also because excessive physical activity could rupture the hymen and so place the matter of a woman's virginity in serious doubt.

Any woman who did not act in appropriate ways would bring shame to her male sponsor. As already noted, she had no honor in her own right to maintain: her role was to help maintain her male sponsor's honor.

Women without male sponsors were an embarrassment to the ancient world. A widow without an extended family in which to be embedded had to become either a prostitute or a beggar: there were no other avenues of acquiring money open to her. This was the case with any single woman who suddenly lost all her male sponsors. This explains why the early church selected widows as their first social responsibility.

The core values of honor and shame are probably the most important to take into account when trying to understand the way people related to each other and their community in the first-century Mediterranean world.

Embedded Identity

We, today, are so used to seeing ourselves as separate individuals with individual rights that we can easily misunderstand people's perceptions of themselves in the ancient world. They had no sense of personal identity the way we do. They did not try to understand the feelings of others either.

Every person was embedded in another person, a family, a tribe, a village, a city, a country. You were known by others as "the son of," "the daughter of," a relative of some head of the family. If you were a visitor from another place, than you were "Jesus of Nazareth," "Saul of Tarsus," "Barnabas of Cyprus," and so on.

If you were not the head of a household, then your actions were seen as either maintaining or damaging the honor of that head and as an important part of the behavior of your family unit. You were not seen as an individual, acting in your own personal right. Wherever you went you were always identified in terms of your father or your place of residence, or both. You always acted as a representative of your family or village, never as yourself alone.

In the Mediterranean world, everyone knew about being a member of a family, a community and a village. This was their personal identity. When a slave was liberated, the slave always took on the name of a family head or of a god, in order to have an identity. A personal identity separate from anyone else was impossible and unthinkable.

When people, either Jews or gentiles, became christians, they took their identity from their new father, God. They saw themselves as members of the family of God, the congregation, with Jesus Christ as their elder brother.

When the head of a household became a follower of Jesus, the whole household, including slaves, would naturally also do so. If a junior member of a household turned to Christ, then there would be division in the household, often resulting in that member being disowned. That person would then often try and join another household who had all turned to Christ, or at least identify with a congregation.

We will never understand how society worked in New Testament times until we come to terms with their lack of individualism, and with the fact that it was always someone else who established a person's identity. This was especially the case with women. Women had no identity as women, only as related to some man. No woman ever saw herself as embedded in her mother or older sister or grandmother or any other woman. Without a male sponsor she had no identity or importance at all.

One of the changes that Jesus brought was to relate to women as though they had an identity as women. He spoke to them directly, never, as was the custom, through a father, husband, brother or son. He accepted their gifts and ministrations in spite of the appearance of shame that such gifts brought him.

We must always be on the lookout for those cases where Jesus went against the customs of his day, and for those cases when he deliberately stayed within the boundaries. When I come to dealing with particular women, I will be taking special note of these things, because they are very important in working out just what was happening in the lives of these Mediterranean people. Jesus himself was a Mediterranean and was brought up in Mediterranean ways. But he saw himself embedded in his father, God, not in his deceased father Joseph.

A World of Limited Good

In Australia we have seen an engine driver become a prime minister; and as Australians we are proud of that, even if we did not particularly like that individual. This could never have happened in the Mediterranean world. It was almost impossible to better the social position into which you were born.

Poor immigrants have arrived in Australia, Canada and the USA, worked hard and done well—sometimes made their fortune and even returned to their home country to live out their lives in luxury. This could never have happened in Jesus' day.

Today, if you have need of a new car, you simply go out and arrange a loan and buy your new car. The equivalent would have been impossible in the first-century Mediterranean world. Even the idea of saving for any item of luxury was a foreign one.

In this century we believe that there is an infinite supply of goods and services. Even if there is a shortage of something, we simply wait awhile and our need is supplied. We can buy almost anything we like by working hard and saving up for it. But in the Mediterranean world, the perception was that everything was in limited supply. And that "everything" included non-tangible items like love, honor, friendship, luck and health. Because of this, then, you must not look to have more than your community said was your right. To try and acquire more furniture or land or sheep or friends or honorable mentions than was appropriate to your status would have been interpreted as your trying to push in ahead of someone else in the status queue, and you would be duly jeered at and dishonored. Likewise, for you to have less than was your due would also have brought you disapprobation.

Your status position was a carefully and precisely determined one, and you moved out of it at your peril.

The only way, then, of becoming rich beyond your status was to take from someone else. This is one reason why the rich are so criticized and despised in the New Testament. The rich became rich only at the expense of the poor. The rich created structural poverty by buying up all the arable land and then forcing peasants to work that land and give most of the fruits of their labor back to the landowners. Men who inherited their riches were held to account because their fathers and grandfathers before them created their wealth out of the poor.

Even friends were perceived to be in limited supply. You stayed within the family and village networks. Any attempt to widen your circle of friends was perceived as trying to win people away from others and their networks.

Honor also was limited. You inherited your honorable position from your father. You could not gain more honor without trying to take someone else's place in the honor stakes. The way honors are distributed annually in some countries today would have been impossible in the Mediterranean world.

The Jews believed that the love of God was limited and belonged solely to them. Gentiles had to become converted to Judaism before they could share in God's love. When Jesus came proclaiming that the love of God was not limited but infinite and available to all who ask for it, he was deliberately going against the perception that everything in the universe was of limited supply.

Many aspects of the way the early christians dealt with social problems can be best understood in the light of the general perception of limited good.

Everything in its Place

Peace and order were perceived to result from everything and everybody being accorded a proper place. In all open societies like those of the Mediterranean world, laws needed to be at a minimum and customs at a maximum. Laws needed to be interpreted by specialists, while customs were imbibed with mother's milk.

So-called "purity" rules have nothing at all to do with our notion of hygiene. If something or someone is "pure," then that thing or person is in their correct place and so does not bring any harm to anyone else. But someone not in his or her proper place is perceived to be a threat to peace and order, and is therefore labeled "impure."

One of the preoccupations of the Mediterranean world was all those fluids that come out of the human body. While they are inside the body they are in their proper place. Once they emerge from the body, they are "out of place" and therefore a

13

potential threat to the good order of the community. Thus blood, pus, urine, feces, saliva, mucus, perspiration, semen, tears, breath would all be regarded as being out of place once they left the body.

Rituals were devised in order to recognize that these things were out of place and to help remove the perceived threat to the order and peace of the community. Jews, like all races at that time, were never sure that other races took the same trouble to deal with these threats to order. This meant that, for example, when a Jew went to the local market to buy a new cooking pot, he would do two things when he returned home: he would ask his wife to wash the pot thoroughly, and he would take off his outer garment, wash it and then put on a new one. Both these things needed to be done because he could never be sure who had picked up the cooking pot or who had brushed against his cloak while he picked his way through the crowds at the market.

When a husband made love to his wife they must both bathe afterwards because his semen had left his body and entered hers, making her "unclean," and because some of his seminal fluid and her natural lubricant would be on his body. There would also be sweat from each on the other, and saliva.

Even birth was a case where the concept of being "out of place" was critical. Here was this new person, in its place inside the mother, now emerging from its mother and being out of place. Elaborate rituals had to be engaged in to deal with the placenta and the fluids that also emerged from the mother's body. The baby had to be initiated into the family. Once all these things had been attended to, the baby was in its place in the family, tribe and village, and the mother in a suitable "clean" condition to resume her place.

The Old Testament describes these rituals for Israelites in Leviticus 12. The mother is to be ritually unclean—not allowed to be with other people—for seven days if the baby is a boy. On the eighth day the baby boy is circumcized and then the mother continues to be regarded as unclean for another thirty-three days. If the baby is a girl, these periods of uncleanness are doubled. At the conclusion of her period of separation from her family, the mother has to bring an offering to the Lord. One can only speculate on why the mother is penalized for giving birth to a female baby.

It is important to reiterate that these "purity" rules had nothing to do with hygiene. They were devised to ensure that the good order of the family and society was not being breached by unwanted intrusions, from whatever source, of matter that belonged inside the human body. Since blood and amniotic fluid could continue to seep from the woman's womb for some time after childbirth, the fixed periods of ritual uncleanness were necessary to ensure that the flow had finally ended.

Another example of dealing with a person out of place is found in Deuteronomy 21:10–14. If an Israelite warrior takes a fancy to a woman he has captured in battle, he can take her to his home and marry her. But he must first shave her head, trim her nails and put new clothes on her. She must mourn her father and mother for a month and then the warrior is free to take her to his bed. As an enemy she is out of place in Israel. If she is to stay in this family, then she has to undergo these indignities as part of the ritual of finding her a place in her new family. These things are all visible to the rest of the family and tribe, so that they, too, can know that she is out of place and therefore not to be welcomed or related to in any way until the rituals are completed.

15

Order could also be breached by people of the same race but from outside the village entering the closed community. When a guest from another village arrived, there were elaborate rituals of greeting which served also to recognize that the guest was from another place and needed to be melded into this community so as not to be a potential threat to their order.

Jews would not enter the property of gentiles for fear of ritual contamination. Jews did not know how gentiles dealt with important things like food, clothing, human relationships and dust. Dust belonged outside on roads and footpaths. It was in place there, but when brought inside a house via the feet, sandals and clothes of people, it was out of place and had to be dealt with. Ritual washing of feet and sometimes putting on an outer garment were examples of dealing with out-of-place dust. A good way to insult someone was to deliberately place something considered unclean onto their garments or inside their house. To spit on someone's face or clothing was an insult, as was the shaking of your dust onto their person.

Each community made its own decisions about what was the proper place for everything and then created rituals for dealing with situations in which out-of-placeness occurred. Animals, birds, reptiles and fish all had their proper place in Jewish life, often based upon the kind of food that entered their bodies. In each case only those animals that fed solely on plant life were classified as acceptable to be eaten. Because pigs grubbed in the ground and ate rats, mice and insects, they were looked upon as potentially dangerous to good order, adding unknowns to the urine and feces of humans.

The notions of "sacred" and "profane" are also based on the concept of being out of place. Any thing or person that belonged to a divinity was in its proper place when used for that divinity; but when used for some other reason was considered to be out of place.

Thus, a utensil that was used for ritual washing during a religious ceremony was regarded as being dedicated for that purpose. If used in some non-religious context, then the divinity was regarded as having been dishonored or blasphemed. Utensils and people that were to be dedicated to a divinity needed to have some ritual performed over them in order to signify that their proper place was now in that sacred service. Elaborate public rituals were devised so that everyone would know the proper place of this utensil or person. If some other utensils or persons were used, not having been set apart for this sacred purpose, then they were regarded as being out of place and not fit for the service of the divinity.

The terms "sacred" and "profane" refer, therefore, to the proper place in which the utensil or person is to operate. It is important to understand here that they do not refer to any inherent moral or spiritual quality of the utensil or person, but simply to the sphere in which each has a proper place.

Nearly all the rules of religious purity mentioned in the gospels are tied to this notion of out-of-placeness. The labels "clean" and "unclean" were convenient ways of referring to what was in place and what out of place, and "sacred" and "profane" to the spheres of activity in which being in place was appropriate.

The Surrogate Family

The family of blood and kin was the foundation of the whole of Mediterranean society. Every person's identity was located within the family. When a younger son left his family to go to the city, he would try and find a family in which to re-embed himself. It would probably have no blood or kinship ties with the extended family he came from. If there were even distant cousins in the city, he would find a natural home with them. This new family was known as his surrogate family. He would now find his new identity there.

It is important to realize that Jesus often talks about the kingdom of God as a surrogate family, with God as the father and himself as the elder brother. All other members are on an equal footing as far as authority is concerned, and they relate to each other pretty much as in a natural family. This becomes important when trying to understand some of Jesus' apparently anti-family sayings. He is merely saying that when there is a conflict between a person's responsibilities to the surrogate kingdom-of-God family and the natural family, then the surrogate family must have first preference.

What will become obvious is that in the surrogate family of the kingdom of God, women cease to be secondary and important only in relationship to a man, and find their identity in their own right as sisters of their elder brother, Christ.

2. Woman in her Place

A great deal has been written about the place of women in the ancient world. I want to concentrate on those aspects of the place of women that help to highlight their situations as reported in the New Testament.

Woman's primary and most important place was in the household. She was required to manage the household budget and see that the household slaves were properly supervised. She had to organize the food and welcome rituals for her husband's dinners. She was responsible for the rearing and education of the children, until the boys came to puberty when the father took over their education and discipline. It was her responsibility to see that nothing or no-one out of place came into the house.

Whenever she left the house to go shopping or visiting those within her natural network, she had to be accompanied by a suitable male, not so much to protect her, but to protect her husband's name from any slips she might make, however inadvertently, through improper conduct. Any males who wished to address her had to do so through her chaperone and not directly. A woman had to be careful when in the company of males that no perceived dishonor to her husband's name could result.

Her body belonged solely to her husband. He alone could touch her and enter her. For any other adult male to do so would bring shame and dishonor to her husband. In this sense she was sacred to him and could be used only by him. Adultery was perceived to be a sin against the husband, whereas a husband was free to touch and enter the body of any unmarried, adult, single female without incurring the charge of adultery. Such an act did not bring any shame or dishonor to him. Should he take the virginity of the daughter of some man of higher social status than him, then that man could sue him for damage to his reputation and honor.

Once reaching puberty, daughters were expected to marry in the order of their age, and suitable husbands would be found by their father, or their elder brother should their father be dead. They had no choice in this matter. They brought with them a dowry commensurate with their father's position of honor in the community. This dowry passed to the ownership of the husband, who had to look after but not spend it. When he died it went to the care of his oldest son.

Jewish women were generally not permitted to go into business or to earn money. Should they do things like taking in washing or do housework, the wages were placed in the hands of the woman's male sponsor, be it father, older brother, husband or oldest son. Any daughters unmarried on the death of both parents had to go to the sponsorship of the nearest male relative, who would look after them. If there were none, then they would have to beg for their living or go into prostitution, unless the village took pity on them.

Women also had to sit separately in the synagogue for worship. At social occasions women were always in the background and had to dress appropriately, that is, according to the social standing of their sponsor.

19

A female slave was rarely manumitted. She would be regarded as the possession of her male owner. Should she marry a fellow slave and he was manumitted, she was not. Her children remained also the property of her owner.

As I will show, Jesus chose to treat women rather differently in many ways, and caused a great deal of confusion in his community. The early church gave women a whole new status, until the end of the first century when women virtually disappeared from church life. (For more detailed information on the place of women in the first century of our era, see those studies referred to in the bibliography.)

It is only when we understand something of the place of women in this society that we can even begin to see just how outrageous Jesus and God were in speaking and relating to women the way they did.

I move now to a detailed study of all the women, named and unnamed, in the New Testament.

Notes
1. Mat. 13:53–8; Mk. 6:1–6, Lk. 4:16–40

PART 2 | *Women in the Gospels*

The four gospels of the New Testament record the actions and sayings of a remarkable number of women, given the general attitude of the day to women. And, with important exceptions, most of these women are respectable and respected within their various social classes. You have only to read ancient writers like Herodotus, Pliny and Pausanias to see the difference. Few women are mentioned, and most of those act in rather shameful ways.

One of the first things you notice about the women in the gospels is that they are named in their own right as persons. Since, as I have already shown, a woman's only identity came from her male sponsor—father, husband, uncle, grandfather, son and so on—she was always named with her sponsor. But the only time women are named in this way in the New Testament is when their sponsor is also an important part of the narrative. Most of the time, the woman is treated as if her name was all that was needed to affirm her identity.

This fact alone shows that Christianity had made an initial, radical move towards giving women a status separate from that of men.

I have divided the women in the gospels into a number of categories in order to show that not only were the leaders of the church, beginning with Jesus himself, affirming the right of women to a separate identity, but also the women themselves were beginning to feel that God had given them a right to assert themselves.

1. Demanding to be Heard

The Syro-Phoenician Woman

> And Jesus went away from there and withdrew to the district of Tyre and Sidon. And behold, a Canaanite woman from that region came out and cried, "Have mercy on me, O Lord, Son of David; my daughter is severely possessed by a demon." But he did not answer her a word. And his disciples came and begged him, saying, "Send her away, for she is crying after us." He answered, "I was sent only to the lost sheep of the house of Israel." But she came and knelt before him, saying, "Lord, help me." And he answered, "It is not fair to take the children's bread and throw it to the dogs." She said, "Yes, Lord, yet even the dogs eat the crumbs that fall from their masters' table." Then Jesus answered her, "O woman, great is your faith! Be it done for you as you desire." And her daughter was healed instantly. (Mat. 15:21–28; also Mk. 7:24–30)

The woman who is described by Mark as a Greek from Syro-Phoenicia, is called a Canaanite by Matthew in order to make her out to be as alien as possible. Matthew was concerned that Mark gave the impression that all gentiles had equal rights with Jews to the ministry of Jesus. So, when telling stories about gentiles having faith, these gentiles must always be unusual in having a special kind of faith in God. So Matthew calls her a Canaanite, making her a member of the most hated of all gentile races, who did the most in ancient times to seduce Israel from her faith in Yahweh.

The Canaanite deities were especially notorious among the Jews for their immoral worship rituals, often using temple prostitutes. Hebrew men were shown as being especially attracted to Canaanite women, probably because of their sexual sophistication. The Hebrew prophets railed more against Canaanite deities than against any others.

Matthew, then, calls her a Canaanite to stress her racial origins in a people who were regarded as the most dangerous of all Israel's enemies. For such a foreigner to have any faith at all in Israel's God was extraordinary: so much so that no-one ought to use her as an example of the way Jesus welcomed all foreigners. Matthew reinforces this by having Jesus say of her that her faith was great. In other words—and the same tactic is used by Matthew in the story of the healing of the Roman centurion's servant or son—this gentile woman, although coming from the most unclean of all gentile nations, has a depth of faith greater than that of most Jews, and this made it possible for Jesus to heal her daughter. Thus, says Matthew, you cannot use gentiles like her to prove that the gospel was made available to all gentiles on the same basis as it was made available to the people of God.

It is interesting to note that when Matthew's gospel was written, gentiles were pouring into the church and swamping the christians who had once been Jews, resulting in these christians losing leadership positions in the congregations. They believed that because they had been the first to come to Christ they should be first in line for leadership positions.

But what is important about this story, especially as told by Matthew, is the way this Canaanite woman went right outside social convention, not only in daring to confront a Jewish male, but in taking over a responsibility that her husband should have exercised. I guess you could reconstruct the scene in that Canaanite home as she bullies and nags her husband, finally storming out to confront the Jewish healer herself. No doubt her husband was a true Canaanite and believed only in his gods, and was not prepared to forsake them in favor of the hated Jewish God. Had it been his son who was sick and he had been sure of Jesus' ability to heal him, maybe it would have been a rather different story. But I doubt that he would have been able to abase himself to the Israelite as his wife was soon to do.

No doubt, also, this woman took heart from the fact that this Jew, Jesus, had left his home territory, Galilee, and had come into her territory of Tyre and Sidon. He and his disciples were now the foreigners, the ones out of place. Jesus did not often leave Jewish territory. Matthew tells us that on this occasion he "withdrew," probably to get away from people who had been troubling him. Mark says that he entered a house, which means that he had some friends in this foreign country, and that he didn't want it known that he was there. But it was not to be.

The reaction of Jesus' disciples is also typical, "Send her away, for she is crying after us." How dare she, this gentile and a woman into the bargain, come unbidden before the Master and ask for what is the right only of the Jews. Women had no right to speak directly to male leaders, either in religion or politics; they had to ask their husband or father or brother or son or uncle to intercede on their behalf. Not only that, but she had come into their space unbidden. There had been no welcome rituals—no acknowledgment that she was out of place in this space, especially in this space occupied by men only. She remained, then, a stranger and a foreigner into the bargain, daring to assert herself as both a woman and a foreigner in space that was sacred to these men. She was behaving like a prostitute.

But this outrageous woman, a foreigner, was more concerned over the health of her daughter than over the social niceties of both Jews and gentiles of her society, and demanded to be heard. She was more concerned over her daughter than over what these Jewish males might think of her. She knew what she was doing, and she dared them to do something about it.

Had Jesus not been there they, no doubt, would have walked away from her and ignored her. They could not physically touch her, for to do so would have been to make themselves ritually unclean—tainted by her out-of-placeness. As it was, they spoke about her to Jesus, and not directly to her. Even to acknowledge her presence to her face would have been to give her a place in their space.

Jesus, not the disciples, hears her, and answers her call for healing for her daughter. She was prepared to be seen as a whore and a social outcast rather than allow an opportunity for the healing of her daughter to pass by.

Jesus at first reinforces her position as being out of place. His place, as an Israelite, was among the people of Israel. He was committed to being their Messiah. Once he left Israel, he was out of place. For him to come to her daughter's aid was to make himself profane. His sacred duty was to Israel: any service to non-Israelites was a non-sacred service. She was asking him to step out of his place and enter her place and exchange his sacredness for hers.

But she persists: "Please, help me Lord!"

Jesus then makes her situation sound even more bleak. "It is not right to take the children's bread and throw it to the dogs."

If you had been that Canaanite mother, you would have recoiled at that stark contrast between the children of the household at the family table and the dogs waiting anxiously outside for the scraps.

Dogs were not kept as pets the way we keep them today in western society. Dogs were almost ownerless, roaming the streets and lanes in packs, scrabbling around rubbish heaps and fighting at doorways during meal times for survival. All dogs were regarded as unclean—out of place in the household, unfit to be touched or handled, useful only for disposing of food scraps and bones. Dogs were thus pariahs—useless, apart from clearing up left-over food. The only exception were those dogs especially bred and trained for tending sheep and goats.

Jesus was likening her to a useless, unwelcome and unclean animal, roaming around the streets, trying to steal what really belonged to the children of the household! But, she was undaunted. She knew that householders used the dogs to get rid of unwanted scraps of food. "True, Lord; but even the dogs are thrown the scraps of food the children leave on the floor."

She was acknowledging what Jesus had put to her; she was out of place in Israel, Jesus' land, and had no right to demand from him what belonged only to his people. To qualify for Jesus' healing, she should first of all become a Jew, and then ask for her daughter to be made well. But she knew, and Jesus knew, that the only way she could become an Israelite was for her husband to convert. Remember a woman's identity flowed from her husband's. The fact that she was there and not her husband was sufficient indication that this was an impossibility.

She was not asking for a new place in Israel. She was asking that, like the dogs who were tolerated but given no proper place in the household, she would be tolerated as a stranger and be thrown a scrap of unwanted bread. She just wanted her daughter to be healed by this Israelite man who she knew was gifted as a healer.

What we see here is a very typical confrontation between two Mediterraneans: one a male Israelite of some authority and reputation, and one a Canaanite foreign woman, out of place in Israelite territory and with no social standing whatsoever.

By accepting her place as defined by Jesus and by asking to be treated as a stray, she caused no trouble for Jesus. She accepted his gift of healing on his terms, even though she had asserted her right to make the first move. What had been a rather dangerous strategy for her turned out to benefit the one she most cared about—her sick daughter.

From Matthew's perspective in writing to assert the priority of Jews over gentiles in the church, her behavior and her faith in Jesus were so outstanding as to be atypical of gentiles, and therefore she could not be used as proof that Jesus welcomed all gentiles into the Messianic family.

Jesus finally gives her her heart's desire, making it clear that he could heal her daughter only because of her outstanding faith in him and because of her clear acknowledgment of her true place as a stranger in Israel with no rights to Israel's Messiah.

The Mother of James and John

> Then the mother of the sons of Zebedee came up to him, with her sons, and kneeling before him she asked him for something. And he said to her, "What do you want?" She said to him, "Command that these two sons of mine may sit, one at your right hand and one at your left, in your kingdom." But Jesus answered, "You do not know what you are asking. Are you able to drink the cup that I am to drink?" They said to him, "We are able." He said to them, "You will drink my cup, but to sit at my right hand and at my left is not mine to grant, but it is for those for whom it has been prepared by my Father." And when the ten heard it, they were indignant at the two brothers. (Mat. 20:20–24; also Mk. 10:35–41)

When James and John had left home to join Jesus they had done a socially unacceptable thing: they had dishonored their father. Zebedee had a large family fishing business and would have been much honored in his village. His eldest son would have been expected to take over this business on his death and thus continue the honored position of the family in the community. He would have been expected to find husbands and dowries for any unmarried sisters and help any

27

unmarried brothers set up their homes, as well as care for his wife and make sure that she had adequate support should he die before her. So when both sons left the business to follow Jesus, they would have been perceived to have acted irresponsibly and to have brought dishonor on their father. On Zebedee's death who would carry on the business and the family honor? The whole village would have been in utter turmoil over such irresponsible behavior, and Zebedee would have been blamed for not having brought up his sons properly. The village would also been upset that its whole reputation had been put at risk by the behavior of these young men.

Jewish men took their role as family head very seriously. The honor of the village with respect to other villages depended to a large extent on the maintenance of family honor by each of its families. The eldest son was not free to leave home and take up a trade or occupation different from his father's. Life choices were severely limited in a world perceived to be of limited resources.

So when these young men responded to the call of Jesus and left home, they not only acted against the will of their father and the expectations of their village; they also brought upon the family name and the village reputation a great amount of dishonor and shame.

Two years later, Jesus is being honored as the Messiah who would soon cast off the yoke of the Roman invaders and restore honor to Israel. Zebedee has gone to his grave in dishonor. This must have been the case, for otherwise there is no way that his wife would have dared to come unbidden before Jesus.

Zebedee's widow decides to do something about restoring honor to her late husband's name. Notice that she is not named, simply referred to as the wife of this well-known fishing entrepreneur. The identity of a wife is embedded in that of her husband, even though he has died. She goes to Jesus, unbidden, kneels before him like a slave—an action outlandish for a woman who was once honored as the wife of Zebedee—and asks that her two sons be made the Messiah's chief assistants in the coming kingdom.

Bear in mind that this happened in public, somewhere out in the open where a great number of people would have seen it. This was not behind closed doors nor in a foreign country, as in the case of the Canaanite woman. And rightly so: this widow had been publicly shamed by her sons' leaving home, and now she wants to regain that honor just as publicly.

But, once again, she is out of her place. Her place is in her home, looking after the household and making sure that it runs smoothly. She can legitimately move outside her place only to do the shopping and perhaps to take some food to a needy neighbor.

Her action in kneeling before Jesus in public is her way of acknowledging that she is out of place here. For her to have stood in Jesus' presence to make her request would have been seen by the bystanders as the action of a person who believed she had social equality with Jesus. For a woman that would have been doubly shameful: women waited to be asked before speaking to a man; and no woman had any honorable position in society apart from her male sponsor.

In asking for her sons to be Jesus' senior assistants she was trying to ensure that her sons would have positions of honor far in excess of those they left behind when they joined Jesus. She wanted to be able to go back to her village in triumph and announce to all and sundry that her sons had acquired greater honor than they had left behind. Thus she would regain—even enhance—her husband's lost honor. And since this would have happened in public, there would have been plenty of male witnesses to attest to her claim. We need to remember that the word of a Jewish woman had no standing

29

at all in Jewish society. Everything had to be attested to by the support of male witnesses.

We must see her act in its social context. Although Jesus went on to show how she was misguided, that in the kingdom of God honor was not a factor in social relationships, he does not criticize her. He knew that her concern was not so much for herself but for the honor of her late husband and for her village. Women did not have positions of honor in that society, so she was not asking anything for herself.

In fact both Matthew and Mark report how Jesus used her shameful behavior to teach his disciples a rather important lesson in honor and leadership. He showed how the male concepts of honor and leadership that drove her to this action would not apply in the kingdom he would establish. True leaders will give up the honor that once went with leadership and take on the social position of the most despised segment of the community—slaves. Leaders will serve like slaves, not rule like lords and masters.

I find it interesting that Mark does not have her asking this of Jesus, but the men themselves. Matthew, you see, wants his men to come out squeaky clean, so he burdens the woman with the blame.

I find myself admiring this widowed mother. Her outrageous behavior on behalf of her family is deserving of far more recognition than it generally finds. Without her, we may never have been given the leadership model that Jesus would enshrine as that to be used by the church.

Anna the Prophet

> And there was a prophetess, Anna, the daughter of Phanuel, of the tribe of Asher; she was of a great age, having lived with her husband seven years from her virginity, and as a widow till she was eighty-four. She did not depart from the temple, worshipping with fasting and prayer night

> and day. And coming up at that very hour she gave thanks
> to God, and spoke of him to all who were looking for the
> redemption of Jerusalem. (Lk. 2:36–38)

When Jesus came to be presented to God in the temple after his circumcision, two people celebrated with Jesus and his parents. One was Simeon, a righteous and devout man who was praying earnestly for the salvation of Israel. God's spirit revealed to him that Jesus was the Messiah, so he took the babe into his arms and prophesied in the words of the song we now call the Nunc Dimittis.

But there was an elderly woman there too. She was from the tribe of Asher, one of the few tribes that had responded to Hezekiah's call to revive the Passover at Jerusalem at a time when the nation was in disarray. She had married as a virgin and lived most of her adult life as a widow, now eighty-four. In those days, widows had to be supported by friends and family, for they would have been unable to earn money for themselves. Luke calls her a prophet. Judaism had no time for women as priests, prophets or queens. In the Old Testament most of the women associated with religion and government were evil.

Anna was too old to take in washing, even if she had been allowed to earn money for herself. But she was not too old to be a prophet. Having come to the temple for Jesus' presentation, "she gave thanks to God and spoke of him to all who were looking for the redemption of Jerusalem." When no-one else in authority was proclaiming the birth of the Messiah, this old woman was telling the world.

How outrageous of her that was! Old women should sit at the back and get on with their prayers and not open their toothless mouths. And no women of whatever age had a right to be saying anything, because no-one would believe them until at least two males agreed with what they were

31

saying. Anna knew that no-one would take much notice of her; but she also knew that inner urge of God's spirit to proclaim the truth that had been given to her. She obeyed God, and that was all that mattered to her. Let people ignore her message at their own peril!

The tribe that once helped restore the Passover to Jerusalem was to have a member prophesying the presence of the Lamb of God who would take away the sins of the whole world.

The Maid who Challenged Peter

> Then they seized him and led him away, bringing him into the high priest's house. Peter followed at a distance; and when they had kindled a fire in the middle of the courtyard and sat down together, Peter sat among them. Then a maid, seeing him as he sat in the light and gazing at him, said, "This man also was with him." But he denied it, saying, "Woman, I do not know him." And a little later some one else saw him and said, "You also are one of them." But Peter said, "Man, I am not." And after an interval of about an hour still another insisted, saying, "Certainly this man also was with him; for he is a Galilean." But Peter said, "Man, I do not know what you are saying." And immediately, while he was still speaking, the cock crowed. (Lk. 22:54–60; also Mat. 26:69–75 and Jn. 18:16–18)

She was a saucy one, the young slavegirl whose job it was to see that visitors doffed their dusty sandals before they entered the high priest's house, washed their feet and made sure that they brought no out-of-place dust inside. She stepped right out of line when she strode up to Peter and accused him of being in league with that traitor Jesus.

Since Peter was out of place in the courtyard of this high priest's house and had come in unbidden, she probably felt it was worth the risk. She would not have dared to behave in this way towards anyone there who had been invited. But she actually started quite a trend, for soon afterwards a couple of men took up the challenge and accused him of being a traitor to Israel.

I wonder whether any of those men would have bothered had this young girl not behaved so outrageously towards a man who may or may not have been a guest of the high priest?

Peter ended up convicting himself of lying and betraying the very master whom he had sworn to follow to the death!

When leaders are allowed to get away with corrupt leadership, it often falls to the lot of outrageous women to tell what they see as the truth, no matter what their station in life. And this woman made no pretence whatsoever of being religious. Notice also that once she had taken such a bold step, two men followed her lead and challenged Peter, resulting in his final downfall and the acknowledgment of his denial of Jesus.

The Samaritan Woman at the Well

Now when the Lord knew that the Pharisees had heard that Jesus was making and baptizing more disciples than John (although Jesus himself did not baptize, but only his disciples), he left Judea and departed again to Galilee. He had to pass through Samaria. So he came to a city of Samaria, called Sychar, near the field that Jacob gave to his son Joseph. Jacob's well was there, and so Jesus, wearied as he was with his journey, sat down beside the well. It was about the sixth hour.

There came a woman of Samaria to draw water. Jesus said to her, "Give me a drink." For his disciples had gone away into the city to buy food. The Samaritan woman said to him, "How is it that you, a Jew, ask a drink of me, a woman of Samaria?" For Jews have no dealings with Samaritans. Jesus answered her, "If you knew the gift of God, and who it is that is saying to you, 'Give me a drink,' you would have asked him, and he would have given you

33

living water." The woman said to him, "Sir, you have nothing to draw with, and the well is deep; where do you get that living water? Are you greater than our father Jacob, who gave us the well, and drank from it himself, and his sons, and his cattle?" Jesus said to her, "Every one who drinks of this water will thirst again, but whoever drinks of the water that I shall give him will never thirst; the water that I shall give him will become in him a spring of water welling up to eternal life." The woman said to him, "Sir, give me this water, that I may not thirst, nor come here to draw."

Jesus said to her, "Go, call your husband, and come here." The woman answered him, "I have no husband." Jesus said to her, "You are right in saying, 'I have no husband'; for you have had five husbands, and he whom you now have is not your husband; this you said truly." The woman said to him, "Sir, I perceive that you are a prophet. Our fathers worshiped on this mountain; and you say that in Jerusalem is the place where men ought to worship." Jesus said to her, "Woman, believe me, the hour is coming when neither on this mountain nor in Jerusalem will you worship the Father. You worship what you do not know; we worship what we know, for salvation is from the Jews. But the hour is coming, and now is, when the true worshipers will worship the Father in spirit and truth, for such the Father seeks to worship him. God is spirit, and those who worship him must worship in spirit and truth." The woman said to him, "I know that Messiah is coming (he who is called Christ); when he comes, he will show us all things." Jesus said to her, "I who speak to you am he." Just then his disciples came. They marveled that he was talking with a woman, but none said, "What do you wish?" or, "Why are you talking with her?" So the woman left her water jar, and went away into the city, and said to the people, "Come, see a man who told me all that I ever did. Can this be the Christ?" They went out of the city and were coming to him.

Meanwhile the disciples besought him, saying, "Rabbi, eat." But he said to them, "I have food to eat of which you do not know." So the disciples said to one another, "Has any one brought him food?" Jesus said to them, "My food is to do the will of him who sent me, and to accomplish his work. Do you not say, 'There are yet four months, then comes the harvest'? I tell you, lift up your eyes, and see how the fields are already white for harvest. He who reaps receives wages, and gathers fruit for eternal life, so that sower and reaper may rejoice together. For here the saying holds true, 'One sows and another reaps.' I sent you to reap that for which you did not labor; others have labored, and you have entered into their labor."

Many Samaritans from that city believed in him because of the woman's testimony, "He told me all that I ever did." So when the Samaritans came to him, they asked him to stay with them; and he stayed there two days. And many more believed because of his word. They said to the woman, "It is no longer because of your words that we believe, for we have heard for ourselves, and we know that this is indeed the Savior of the world." (Jn. 4:1–42)

This woman had everything against her. She was a Samaritan. No Jewish male would dare be seen talking to a Samaritan man, let alone a woman. Samaritans, you see, had betrayed the true faith of Israel by marrying foreign women and then setting up their own temple on Mount Gerizim. But she was also a bad woman. She had had five husbands—fortunately for her not all at the same time—and was now living in sin with a sixth man. This was why she came in the middle of the day to collect water from the village well, knowing that there would be no other women there to accuse her of being a sinner.

Jesus was once again out of place in foreign territory. This was Samaria, and Jews avoided Samaria like the plague. When Jesus arrived at the well, he must have known why she was there at that time of the day. Indeed we know that because he talked about her having had five husbands.

When he asked her for some water, she quite outrageously criticized him for daring to talk to her since he knew she was a Samaritan. Had she behaved as befitted any woman in such circumstances, she would not have made any reply to this person—a male, a foreigner. She would simply have acceded to his request and given him a drink of water. But she was an outcast in her own village, and she probably felt that she had nothing more to lose, so she gave vent to her feelings.

Soon she and Jesus were engaged in some rather heavy theology, until she finally realized that he must be the true Messiah. It is interesting to read John's account of this conversation and to notice how well she had listened to the men in her life when they discussed religious issues. She would not have been allowed to do more than listen, as women were discouraged from taking an interest in the faith. Yet she could say to Jesus, "I know that Messiah is coming and that he will show us all things."

When Jesus told her that he was that very Messiah she rushed back to her village, risked the ire and jeering of the people, and shouted to all and sundry that she had just been talking with the Messiah. That whole village turned to their Messiah that day, and all because an outrageous woman demanded to be heard, both by the Messiah and by the village that despised her.

But notice how in the end the Samaritan men downplayed her part in their recognition of Jesus as Messiah: "It is no longer because of your words that we believe, for we have heard for ourselves, and we know that this is indeed the Savior of the world." This is a reminder that in a Jewish court the testimony of a woman needs the corroborative testimony of several men before it can be accepted. Court cases in our own day involving battered wives remind us that little has changed!

These five women, then, are typical of the way some women stood outside their social position in this male-dominated society and demanded to be listened to. They had needs too; they had important things to say; they helped run the family and the village and were prepared to go directly to Jesus with a sure instinct that he would most certainly listen to them and give them a fair hearing.

In each case they were rewarded with their request answered or their message heard.

2. Demanding the Right to be Ministered to

The next group of women represent those who came to Jesus with personal needs. The previous group came with requests for others, but these women had to step even more out of line, for only their male sponsors had any right to make requests on their behalf.

The Woman with the Issue of Blood

> And a woman who had had a flow of blood for twelve years and could not be healed by anyone, came up behind him, and touched the fringe of his garment; and immediately her flow of blood ceased. And Jesus said, "Who was it that touched me?" When all denied it, Peter said, "Master, the multitudes surround you and press upon you!" But Jesus said, "Someone touched me; for I perceive that power has gone forth from me." And when the woman saw that she was not hidden, she came trembling, and falling down before him declared in the presence of all the people why she had touched him, and how she had been immediately healed. And he said to her, "Daughter, your faith has made you well; go in peace." (Lk. 8:43–48; also Mat. 9:20–22 and Mk. 5:25–34)

This woman was caught in an absolutely no-win situation. Any person, male or female, who was suffering from an illness that resulted in any emission of fluids of any kind from the body, was labeled "unclean" and was not allowed to make social contact with other people and was especially forbidden to attend worship in synagogue and temple. These body fluids were now considered out of place and had to be dealt with in case of any risk to the good order of the community. There were elaborate rituals to be done in the sight of the family—washings and reclothing—before normal social mixing was possible.

All societies define what is safe for their members and in

the process devise ways of protecting themselves from those people who act outside those safety rules, as I have already discussed in part 1. In the Jewish society of Jesus' days, only a person with a whole body was a completely safe person with whom others could relate. A man with crushed testicles or a missing hand, for example, was not allowed to serve in the temple or synagogue.

Emissions from any part of the body rendered a person a danger to the welfare of the community. Such persons had to be marked and excluded: they were thus labeled "unclean," or out of place, mostly for religious and political reasons. A husband and wife engaging in sexual intercourse were doing a perfectly normal and natural thing. But because semen had been emitted from his body into hers, both were in an unsafe condition. This was corrected by having a bath as soon as possible afterwards, thus making them in a safe condition to mix with the rest of the community. (I have often pictured to myself the Israelite men during the forty years wandering in the wilderness debating the worthwhileness of making love to their wives regularly when they had to spend so much of their physical energy in carrying enough water around the desert to make such activity possible!)

It was because Jews could not be too sure about how gentiles dealt with emissions of fluid from their bodies that they labeled all gentiles unclean. Public washing and reclothing were required of any gentiles who wished to become members of a Jewish community. In the case of men this also involved their undergoing circumcision.

I have gone into some detail about this so that you can see just how outrageous was the behavior of the woman with the issue of blood. We tend to think of her as having some kind of continual menstruation, whereas the blood could have been coming from anywhere in her body. It could have resulted from an ulcer that continually exuded blood. This permanent emission of blood meant that she could not sleep with her husband, if she had one; could not cook for her children, if she had any; could not go shopping; she could not go to the synagogue and temple to ask God for healing. She was in a state of total alienation from her family and the community, and from God.

When this nameless woman forced her way through the crowds following Jesus to the house of Jairus, leader of the synagogue, and dared to touch Jesus' garment, she was breaking every social convention. She would have been well known. Certainly Jairus would have known her as it was his responsibility to see that such people did not gain entrance to his synagogue. Every person in that crowd she touched would have been made unclean, and when she touched Jesus she made him unclean for seven days.

Her behavior was outrageous in the extreme. But she was desperate. No physicians had been able to help her over the years. She could not get access to priests or healers in the temple. Only Jesus could bring her back into the community. And she dared the wrath of the community, who could well have lynched her in anger at such temerity.

But notice Jesus' attitude. He did not once challenge her for breaking the social conventions. He did not once condemn her for making him unclean and therefore unfit to go ahead and heal Jairus' daughter.

What he did was to force her to identify herself publicly before the crowd. He then confirmed that she no longer had this emission of blood. "Go in peace" is very expressive here, for it says to all around that no uncleanness had been imparted to anyone, not even to himself. The community was healed and made whole too. Both she and everyone she had brushed against were restored to social and religious safety.

He had felt healing power flow out of his body and into hers. This process ensured that social norms were irrelevant—

even dehumanizing. The healing power of God bows to no human convention when the life and well-being of a single believer is threatened.

The outrageous behavior of this woman is a sign to us that our outrageous exclusion of women from equal fellowship in the church will be met with outrageous reactions of women as they struggle for recognition and equality. Too often we force people to behave in ways that we label "selfish," when all the time we are marginalizing them and forcing them to take actions we call "unsocial."

Mary and Martha, the Sisters of Lazarus

> Now as they went on their way, he entered a village; and a woman named Martha received him into her house. And she had a sister called Mary, who sat at the Lord's feet and listened to his teaching. But Martha was distracted with much serving; and she went to him and said, "Lord, do you not care that my sister has left me to serve alone? Tell her then to help me." But the Lord answered her, "Martha, Martha, you are anxious and troubled about many things; one thing is needful. Mary has chosen the good portion, which shall not be taken away from her." (Lk. 10:38–42)

Jesus did an outrageous thing: he went into a house where he would be alone with two unmarried women! That was very much a no-no among Jews in those days. Two men could be alone in a house with one woman, but not the other way around. That's how much men feared the sexual power of women! Doesn't it remind you of some of the rhetoric of the men who shudder at the idea of a woman at the altar and in the pulpit and what thoughts she will engender in the minds of the men in the pews?

But there Jesus was in that small village of Bethany, alone in the house with Martha and Mary. Everyone in that village would have seen him go in. Knowing that Lazarus, their brother, was away on business, the curious would have found some excuse to go walking past the house and gaze through window and door to see what might be going on inside!

Any decent woman would either have asked him to leave and come back later when Lazarus was back, or at least have stayed on her feet and kept moving about so as to make it quite clear that nothing untoward was going on. But no! Look at Mary! She sat herself down on the floor at Jesus' feet and listened attentively while he taught her.

No wonder that Martha panicked! She flew round the house making as much noise as she could to distract the neighbors, hoping her stupid sister would get the message and get to her feet and save their reputation!

But no! She stayed where she was.

Finally, Martha could bear it no longer and turned on Jesus for allowing them to be in this most awkward situation. She didn't really care a lepta for the housework that needed doing—she had probably washed the dishes four times by then! But she did care for the reputation of her family. Jesus knew what was really troubling her and did not take her implied criticism of him unkindly. After all it was he who had breached the social etiquette.

"Martha, Martha! Calm down! Forget about these stupid social niceties! It is more important to understand the truths of the kingdom than it is to know which way to spoon out your soup!

"Mary can't concentrate on listening to me while doing things the way you can. She needs to give me her full attention in order to learn from me. You can listen and do the housework at the same time. I don't care which way you listen, as long as you listen and learn and carry out what I teach you. I'm certainly not going to force Mary to listen with only half an ear because you worry too much about what people will think."

Both the women were outrageous in their own way. Martha in not asking Jesus to leave, and Mary in risking her reputation and her sister's by sitting quietly at his feet.

There are times when the social niceties have to be discarded, when people's lives and souls are more at risk through keeping to society's rules.

Martha and Mary Again

Now a certain man was ill, Lazarus of Bethany, the village of Mary and her sister Martha. It was Mary who anointed the Lord with ointment and wiped his feet with her hair, whose brother Lazarus was ill. So the sisters sent to him, saying, "Lord, he whom you love is ill." But when Jesus heard it he said, "This illness is not unto death; it is for the glory of God, so that the Son of God may be glorified by means of it."

Now Jesus loved Martha and her sister and Lazarus. So when he heard that he was ill, he stayed two days longer in the place where he was. Then after this he said to the disciples, "Let us go into Judea again." The disciples said to him, "Rabbi, the Jews were but now seeking to stone you, and are you going there again?" Jesus answered, "Are there not twelve hours in the day? If any one walks in the day, he does not stumble, because he sees the light of this world. But if any one walks in the night, he stumbles, because the light is not in him." Thus he spoke, and then he said to them, "Our friend Lazarus has fallen asleep, but I go to awake him out of sleep." The disciples said to him, "Lord, if he has fallen asleep, he will recover." Now Jesus had spoken of his death, but they thought that he meant taking rest in sleep. Then Jesus told them plainly, "Lazarus is dead; and for your sake I am glad that I was not there, so that you may believe. But let us go to him." Thomas, called the Twin, said to his fellow disciples, "Let us also go, that we may die with him."

Now when Jesus came, he found that Lazarus had already been in the tomb four days. Bethany was near Jerusalem, about two miles off, and many of the Jews had come to Martha and Mary to console them concerning their brother. When Martha heard that Jesus was coming, she went and met him, while Mary sat in the house. Martha said to Jesus, "Lord, if you had been here, my brother would not have died. And even now I know that whatever you ask from God, God will give you." Jesus said to her, "Your brother will rise again." Martha said to him, "I know that he will rise again in the resurrection at the last day." Jesus said to her, "I am the resurrection and the life; he who believes in me, though he die, yet shall he live, and whoever lives and believes in me shall never die. Do you believe this?" She said to him, "Yes, Lord; I believe that you are the Christ, the Son of God, he who is coming into the world."

When she had said this, she went and called her sister Mary, saying quietly, "The Teacher is here and is calling for you." And when she heard it, she rose quickly and went to him. Now Jesus had not yet come to the village, but was still in the place where Martha had met him. When the Jews who were with her in the house, consoling her, saw Mary rise quickly and go out, they followed her, supposing that she was going to the tomb to weep there. Then Mary, when she came where Jesus was and saw him, fell at his feet, saying to him, "Lord, if you had been here, my brother would not have died." When Jesus saw her weeping, and the Jews who came with her also weeping, he was deeply moved in spirit and troubled; and he said, "Where have you laid him?" They said to him, "Lord, come and see." Jesus wept. So the Jews said, "See how he loved him!" But some of them said, "Could not he who opened the eyes of the blind man have kept this man from dying?"

Then Jesus, deeply moved again, came to the tomb; it was a cave, and a stone lay upon it. Jesus said, "Take away the stone." Martha, the sister of the dead man, said to him, "Lord, by this time there will be an odor, for he has been dead four days." Jesus said to her, "Did I not tell you that if you would believe you would see the glory of God?" So they took away the stone. And Jesus lifted up his eyes and said, "Father, I thank thee that thou hast heard me. I knew that thou hearest me always, but I have said this on account of the people standing by, that they may believe that thou didst send me." When he had said this, he cried with a loud voice, "Lazarus, come out." The dead man came out, his hands and feet bound with bandages, and

43

> his face wrapped with a cloth. Jesus said to them, "Unbind him, and let him go." Many of the Jews therefore, who had come with Mary and had seen what he did, believed in him. (Jn. 11:1–45)

Their brother Lazarus, their breadwinner, was seriously ill. Martha and Mary sent a message to Jesus asking him to come and heal him. But Jesus delayed and Lazarus died.

Martha, the older sister, comes out to meet Jesus, leaving Mary in the house. Lazarus has already been buried.

"Lord, if you had been here our brother would not have died."

I remind you here that women without men found it almost impossible to exist in that society. Any woman who took in washing or did some form of work was not paid directly. The money was given to her male sponsor: a husband or a son or a father or an uncle. Unattached women were an embarrassment to the ancient world. You have to read the passage about widows in 1 Tim. 5 in the light of the fact that these young widows, if not members of an extended family, had only one way they could support themselves directly—prostitution. With no man to accept the wages of her labor, a single, unattached woman was not able to keep herself.

Martha and Mary were now in this predicament. Without their brother they could not earn their own living, keep their house and social respect.

Jesus will raise Lazarus to life for their sake, not for his: after all, Lazarus is far better off in Abraham's bosom, is he not?

Martha's rebuke of Jesus is outrageous, even if true. She tempers this rebuke with the hope that Jesus will restore their brother to them. "Lord, if you had been here, my brother would not have died. And even now I know that whatever you ask from God, God will give you." She knew that she and her family had a special relationship with Jesus that allowed her to express herself in this way, even in public. But there would have been many onlookers who would have gasped, her outspokenness being regarded as not proper for any decent woman.

She then returned home and sent Mary to Jesus. Mary greeted Jesus with the same rebuke, "If you had been here our brother would not have died." And she wept openly.

John states clearly that all the community gathered there were weeping too. They were weeping for the two women who now faced the rest of their lives manless and entirely dependent on the generosity of their village.

Martha's confession that "I believe that you are the Christ, the Son of God" is in itself an outrageous statement, since what women believed was not valued at all in that society.

But from their outrageousness came the miracle of the resurrection of Lazarus and the famous statement, "I am the resurrection and the life."

When Lazarus emerged from the tomb, still bound with the grave clothes soaked in ointment and precious balm, Jesus commanded that these be removed. It would have been his sisters who would have done that, and given him a robe to wear until he reached their home.

This family were once again reunited, the two sisters safe in the sponsorship of their brother, free to take up their roles in the life of their village.

It was during this incident that Jesus himself shed tears—the only time he did so in the whole of his mission. Those tears were in response to the tears of the two sisters who, in their own way, were appealing to him to help them escape a life of bitterness, poverty and shame. Their faith in him was not misplaced, as will not be the faith of any women who need to be rescued from social structures that oppress and punish them for being women.

Martha and Mary a Third Time

> Six days before the Passover, Jesus came to Bethany, where Lazarus was, whom Jesus had raised from the dead. There they made him a supper; Martha served, and Lazarus was one of those at table with him. Mary took a pound of costly ointment of pure nard and anointed the feet of Jesus and wiped his feet with her hair; and the house was filled with the fragrance of the ointment. But Judas Iscariot, one of his disciples (he who was to betray him), said, "Why was this ointment not sold for three hundred denarii and given to the poor?" This he said, not that he cared for the poor but because he was a thief, and as he had the money box he used to take what was put into it. Jesus said, "Let her alone, let her keep it for the day of my burial. The poor you always have with you, but you do not always have me." (Jn. 12:1–8)

After the raising of Lazarus from the grave, Martha and Mary wanted to do something to express their heartfelt thanks at having their life and their brother given back to them. So they decided to give Jesus a feast. But it would have been Lazarus who issued the actual invitation. Martha served. There was, no doubt, a whole day of preparation for this feast. We can only imagine what food would have been served. Both sisters would have spent the whole day in excited preparation, putting all their love into this meal.

John does not tell us about any guests being invited except the twelve disciples. Jesus reclines next to Lazarus, the head of the household. This makes him seated at the place of honor, rather different from the lowest place that was to be given when he went to the house of Simon the pharisee, as you will see. In this case, Jesus would have been given the correct greeting, his sandals taken off, his feet washed and his hair anointed with a sweet smelling oil.

But during the meal, Mary came in. She would not have been seated with the men but would have been out in the kitchen helping Martha. Only Martha actually came into the dining area to serve the men. There would have been fourteen all told—Jesus, Lazarus and the twelve.

Mary brings in some very expensive ointment of pure nard and anoints Jesus' feet, wiping it evenly over them with her long hair. The whole house is filled with the exotic fragrance. That Mary would come in uninvited and perform this ritual was really quite outrageous, even in this family.

The reaction of Judas Iscariot, Jesus' ultimate betrayer, was predictable. He had assumed control of the finances of Jesus' mission, and apparently siphoned some of it off into his own pocket. It was inevitable that he would miss the significance of Mary's action and think only of what he saw as a waste of money: the ultimate economic rationalist!

But Jesus was not going to be sidetracked. He appreciated Mary's gesture. She it was who had sat at Jesus' feet some weeks earlier and had listened as he taught her about the coming kingdom of God and his part in it. Her response in anointing his feet—symbol of action and purpose—was an affirmation that she really did believe that he was "the resurrection and the life." Once resurrected from the grave he would need his feet to move around his new kingdom. Jesus went on to tell Judas that she must be allowed to keep the ointment that was left over so that she could anoint the rest of his body after his death.

Martha and Mary once again demonstrate that Jesus is happy with women who maintain their traditional roles—as Martha did—and with those who believe they should step out and make their own personal statement of faith—as Mary did.

The Crippled Woman

> Now he was teaching in one of the synagogues on the sabbath. And there was a woman who had had a spirit of infirmity for eighteen years; she was bent over and could not fully straighten herself. And when Jesus saw her, he called

her and said to her, "Woman, you are freed from your infirmity." And he laid his hands upon her, and immediately she
was made straight, and she praised God. But the ruler of
the synagogue, indignant because Jesus had healed on
the sabbath, said to the people, "There are six days on
which work ought to be done; come on those days and be
healed, and not on the sabbath day." Then the Lord
answered him, "You hypocrites! Does not each of you on
the sabbath untie his ox or his ass from the manger, and
lead it away to water it? And ought not this woman, a
daughter of Abraham whom Satan bound for eighteen
years, be loosed from this bond on the sabbath day?" As
he said this, all his adversaries were put to shame; and all
the people rejoiced at all the glorious things that were done
by him. (Lk. 13:10–17)

This woman had been bent over double for eighteen years.
Luke calls this condition "a spirit of infirmity," indicating that
the community regarded her as demon-possessed. This meant
that she was ineligible to attend the temple and the synagogue. No-one, man or woman, with any physical disability
was supposed to appear before the Lord in public worship.
Such people were labeled "unclean." They were out of place
in a building dedicated to the worship of God.

When Luke indicates that Jesus "saw her" he probably
means that she used to hide herself among the women in the
gallery or at the back of the synagogue where women were
isolated from the men. She needed to be careful that the
leader of the synagogue did not see her, for he would have
had her removed. Jesus thus deliberately went looking for
her, knowing that she was there.

He called out to her while he was teaching from the scripture, "Woman, you are freed from your infirmity!" This sud-
den outburst was bad enough. That he would speak directly
to a woman and a crippled woman who had no right to be
there in the first place was bad enough, but that he then
broke the sabbath law by performing the work of a healer

and casting out her spirit of infirmity was the very limit! The synagogue head made the assumption that Jesus was a professional healer, and therefore his act of healing was work and thus a breach of sabbath law.

No wonder the ruler of the synagogue was upset. But he did not dare to criticize Jesus, you notice. He turned to the congregation, berated them and told them to come on the weekdays and not on the sabbath if they wanted to be healed. He was primarily upset that he had not seen this woman sneak in, and suspected that some men in the congregation had helped her. This means that there were times during the week when those with disabilities could come and seek help from healers, but not on the sabbath during worship. There would have been no other buildings in the towns where healers could have been sought out for consultation.

Jesus soon put paid to that argument by pointing out that every man present untied his ox or ass to take it out to water it on the sabbath, as on every other day—and wasn't that doing work? He then called her "a daughter of Abraham." They had all regarded her as shameful, you see, because of her demon-possession. They would never have referred to her as the wife of or the daughter of some man because to do so was to bring shame to the man named. But Jesus named Abraham as her father, thus removing any notion of shame from her. He not only healed her, but he removed her shame in the eyes of the community; he was also declaring her right to be there among them in their synagogue.

Her being in the synagogue during a sabbath service was outrageous in the extreme; but the woman knew her rights before God.

Luke adds a wonderful touch to end this story. "All his adversaries were put to shame; and all the people rejoiced at all the glorious things that were done by him."

49

These four women represent those women who believed that they had the right to call upon Jesus for help to overcome personal problems and sickness. They believed that Jesus would not take any notice of the social conventions that marginalized them and prevented them from taking steps to help themselves.

When men fail in their duty to help those very people they have made second-class citizens, then sometimes those women need to go public and risk the ire of their menfolk in order to find the healing and peace that they know has been promised them by God.

3. Demanding the Right to Serve

Women were generally not permitted to take up leadership roles in the community. Their roles were carefully defined as being within the household. There they did have some autonomy over household matters, the cooking and house-keeping, and the care of young children. But when it came to service to the community, only males were allowed that right and privilege. Any public service performed by women had to be channeled through their men and brought acknowledgment only to the man.

The following examples show Jesus approving of those women who chose to serve in their own right.

The Indigent Widow

And he sat down opposite the treasury, and watched the multitude putting money into the treasury. Many rich people put in large sums. And a poor widow came, and put in two copper coins, which make a penny. And he called his disciples to him, and said to them, "Truly, I say to you, this poor widow has put in more than all those who are contributing to the treasury. For they all contributed out of their abundance; but she out of her poverty has put in everything she had, her whole living." (Mk. 12:41–44 and Lk. 21:1–4)

The Jews did not allow into the temple anything that bore any kind of representation of a human form. Gentile money was automatically excluded because it always carried on it the head of the reigning caesar and often the head of a pagan god.

Because only Roman and Greek coins were legal tender in the marketplace, the Jews were allowed to mint their own money for use within the temple. Only Jewish money could be used for offerings to God. These coins had no representation of humans or deities on them. To accommodate the need for worshipers to change their Roman money into temple money, the temple authorities set up exchange booths at the entrance to the temple. Thus worshipers could bring their offerings in Roman money and exchange them for temple money at the door. This was, by the way, a lucrative business for the high priests who alone licensed these money dealers!

The widow who put two copper coins into the treasury— a large chest set up at the entrance so that all could display how much they were giving to the temple—was acting quite outrageously on two accounts: she dared to put in such a small amount and think that God would be pleased; but she dared to put in Roman money!

These copper coins that the gospels mention were of such a small denomination that it was impractical for the Jews to mint equivalent temple money, so she was not able to exchange these two lepta. Since this was all she had, she placed them in the treasury as her offering to God.

This outrageous act would have stunned all the onlookers, especially the treasurer when he came to empty the box and count the coins. Watching the rich and famous flash the money they were putting into the treasury box was a popular pastime on sabbath days. But Jesus commended her outrageousness: "She has put in more than all those who are contributing to the treasury."

Not only did this widow put in all she had in the world; she put in what was unacceptable to the men who ran the temple.

It is more than time that women themselves determined what is right for them to commit to God, and not just what the male hierarchy decides what, if anything, is an appropriate ministry for women in the church.

The Woman who Anointed Jesus

> Now when Jesus was at Bethany in the house of Simon the leper, a woman came up to him with an alabaster flask of very expensive ointment, and she poured it on his head, as he sat at table. But when the disciples saw it, they were indignant, saying, "Why this waste? For this ointment might have been sold for a large sum, and given to the poor." But Jesus, aware of this, said to them, "Why do you trouble the woman? For she has done a beautiful thing to me. For you always have the poor with you, but you will not always have me. In pouring this ointment on my body she has done it to prepare me for burial. Truly, I say to you, wherever this gospel is preached in the whole world, what she has done will be told in memory of her." (Mat. 26:6–13 and Mk. 14:3–9)

The woman who gatecrashed a feast and anointed Jesus with costly ointment is probably a different one from the Mary of Luke's gospel who does the same thing, and the unnamed woman who also arrived, uninvited, at a feast, but in the house of Simon the Pharisee. But the outrageousness of their actions is the same.

Picture the scene.

The village is Bethany, a rather small community where everyone knew everyone else's business. Jesus has been invited to a meal in the house of Simon the leper, so named because he was the Simon who had been cured of his leprosy.

There they were—all the men reclining on couches set around the walls, feasting away as the slavewomen served them and wiped their chops, picked up their discarded scraps and kept their chalices full of wine mixed with water. All the doors and windows were wide open so the whole village could see how sumptuously Jesus was being entertained.

And then a hush.

This unnamed woman comes boldly through the open front door, goes straight to where Jesus is reclining, kneels down at his feet, breaks open a casket of expensive ointment, pours it over Jesus' head and feet, and smooths it out with her long unbraided hair while weeping.

A couple of Jesus' disciples are angry at the dishonor this woman has brought to the Master. They dared not voice their real feelings as this would be seen as a criticism of their Master, so they blurt out something about such sinful waste of money that could have been used to feed the poor. What hypocrisy! They had not given the poor a single thought before then!

And what did such outrageous behavior provoke from Jesus?

"Leave her be! You'll have plenty of time to think about the poor when I'm dead and gone. This woman is anointing my body to prepare me for my coming painful death. Long after all of you have been gone and forgotten, this woman's brave and unselfish action will be celebrated."

53

This outrageous deed of a first-century woman demonstrates quite clearly that what matters is what is in the deepest hearts of women; for it is from the depths of the heart that one's true character emerges.

Yes, the motive and the deed may be outrageous, but God sees where they come from, and responds justly and compassionately.

The Prostitute who Anointed Jesus

One of the Pharisees asked him to eat with him, and he went into the Pharisee's house, and took his place at table. And behold, a woman of the city, who was a sinner, when she learned that he was at table in the Pharisee's house, brought an alabaster flask of ointment, and standing behind him at his feet, weeping, she began to wet his feet with her tears, and wiped them with the hair of her head, and kissed his feet, and anointed them with the ointment.

Now when the Pharisee who had invited him saw it, he said to himself, "If this man were a prophet, he would have known who and what sort of woman this is who is touching him, for she is a sinner." And Jesus answering said to him, "Simon, I have something to say to you." And he answered, "What is it, Teacher?" "A certain creditor had two debtors; one owed five hundred denarii, and the other fifty. When they could not pay, he forgave them both. Now which of them will love him more?" Simon answered, "The one, I suppose, to whom he forgave more."

And he said to him, "You have judged rightly." Then turning toward the woman he said to Simon, "Do you see this woman? I entered your house, you gave me no water for my feet, but she has wet my feet with her tears and wiped them with her hair. You gave me no kiss, but from the time I came in she has not ceased to kiss my feet. You did not anoint my head with oil, but she has anointed my feet with ointment. Therefore I tell you, her sins, which are many, are forgiven, for she loved much; but he who is forgiven little, loves little." And he said to her, "Your sins are forgiven." Then those who were at table with him began to say among themselves, "Who is this, who even forgives sins?" And he said to the woman, "Your faith has saved you; go in peace." (Lk. 7:36–50)

54

This is certainly not the same woman who went to Simon the leper's house. Many of the circumstances are different, and give us an opportunity to look more closely at the place of women in that society.

But first, what was Simon the Pharisee up to when he

invited Jesus to a feast? Did he have some hidden agenda? Was he looking to make a fool of Jesus?

We need to have some idea of what went on at one of the main rituals used by upper-class Jews as a way of maintaining their honor and status in their community.

In the first place, as I have already shown, only people perceived to be of equal status were generally invited to your house for a meal. These meals were part of the reciprocal relationships of this community: you invited only those who could invite you to their home in return, so their home must reflect the same standard as yours, otherwise you would demean yourself by entering a lower-status house. To invite someone of a higher status than you was a risk, because that person may refuse and you would be publicly shamed.

Eating together implied shared ideals and values, and therefore where one sat, who prepared what food with what utensils was of great concern to this community. There were two main stages to a formal meal. The first was conducted near the entrance to the house; one slave saw to the rituals of removing the dusty sandals of the guests and washing their feet in cool water, another anointed their heads with fragrant oil, while another one or two served the guests with appetizers.

After these initial ceremonies, the guests went to the dining room where they reclined in carefully placed order on couches on three sides of the room while being served with their main meal. Scraps of bread were used to wipe the mouth and fingers and then thrown onto the floor for the slaves to gather up and give to the dogs that usually gathered at the door.

Everything had to be done perfectly to avoid adverse comment. The honor of the host was very much at stake here. Subjects for discussion were also carefully selected to minimize argumentation and preserve decorum. And, it goes without saying, only males were invited to such feasts.

The women of the household would have been seen only when serving the guests, and they stayed in the kitchen until called upon.

It was to such a feast that Simon the Pharisee invited Jesus.

At first glance, then, it would seem that Simon the Pharisee recognized Jesus as being on an equal footing with himself. This could have been assumed by the mere fact of the invitation. But as we read further, we soon discover that Jesus was not given the introductory courtesies. His feet were not washed and his head not anointed with oil. He was not even given the formal introductory kiss on the cheek normally given to all guests.

So—what were Simon's intentions?

There was, in fact, no way that a rich Pharisee like Simon would have accepted Jesus as being of his own status. Jesus had been an artisan—a carpenter—and therefore well down the social scale. Jesus had also dishonored his family by leaving his widowed mother and unmarried sisters to care for themselves.

The other guests Simon had invited would have been mortally offended at having such a person as Jesus reclining near them and would not have invited Simon to their home. Indeed, as soon as Jesus was spied, many would have walked off in a huff and thus shamed Simon.

What Simon did was to instruct his slaves to escort Jesus directly to his assigned place at the lowest end of the couches, thus signaling to the other guests that Jesus was to be an object of scorn. Simon and his guests would have been able to say what they wanted to Jesus without threatening their own status and honor. But, in fact, they would only do that if Jesus first drew attention to this lack of courtesy and asked why he had been treated so badly. This would then have opened the way for all the guests and Simon, as host, to assert their higher status.

These games of challenge and response were very craftily played in this community. You only took notice of someone of lower status when they first challenged you. To make the first move against someone below you was to risk losing the argument and being publicly shamed. If someone of lower status challenged you, you simply ignored the challenge and walked away, thus showing your superiority.

In this situation, how did Jesus react? He said and did nothing. He went quietly and in a dignified manner to his place without protest. He cared little for these status games. He did not care how others ranked him, for he knew who he was and what God thought of him, and that was all that mattered. He was often to subvert their games of challenge and response and turn their notions of honor and shame upside down.

Feasts were never held in secret; this was an open society. Everybody knew everybody else's business, especially since no-one was considered simply as an individual. Each person was embedded in a family, a tribe, a village, an area. Since feasts were part of the honor maintenance system, it was in the host's interest to publish abroad his guest list. This was a way of letting some people know that they had not been invited.

So, this prostitute—quite well-known, of course, since it was a rather public profession in those days—would have heard that Jesus was going to be at this feast. Now she would have known something of the mentality of all those guests, since she had probably serviced most of them at one time or another. She would have known how Jesus would be treated, and no doubt set out to get her own back on those pretentious men who claimed such high honor and moral rectitude.

Since the meal proper had started, there was no slave on duty at the entrance to do the washing of feet of guests. And since doors were never closed during the day so that passers-by could see how lavishly the host had feted his guests, the prostitute had no difficulty in entering the house. She went straight in and knew exactly where to find Jesus—at the bottom of the status line.

She stood behind the couch and reached over to where Jesus' feet were just over the edge. She did not face him, for that would have been to cause offense to him. (Remember in the house of Martha and Mary, how Mary sat at Jesus' feet, facing him, for she was a good woman and not a prostitute?) She then took off his sandals, bathed his dusty feet with her tears, wiped them with her hair and kissed them, and then anointed them with fragrant oil.

Notice her tears. They are out of place, and therefore a cause of ritual uncleanness. Her tears falling on Jesus caused him to be ritually unclean, thus making it dangerous for all the other guests who might now brush up against him. Should he now place his hand into a plate of food he would make it unclean and therefore inedible. In such an event the whole gathering would have erupted into a loud protest. Many guests would have immediately got up and left had not Jesus started to talk to Simon, the host.

This prostitute knew exactly what she was doing. She knew how Jesus would have been treated by Simon, and she had decided to make her own protest on behalf of someone who had shown a deep understanding of women who had had no option but to turn to prostitution in order to survive in this male world. (We must always remember that women without male kin to be their sponsors had no way of earning their own living except by prostitution. It was not that Jewish women turned easily to prostitution, far from it.)

She believed that her action was in better taste than Simon's and would be a brave way of showing up the hypocrisy of all these men who were about to try and mock Jesus.

Luke gives us Simon's silent response to this outrage: "If he were a prophet, he would have known who and what sort of woman this is who is touching him."

This gives us an important clue about why Simon invited Jesus in the first place. He wanted to play games with Jesus and test out his ability to know the future and read people's minds. Now we can get a glimpse of the kind of games these guests were soon to play on Jesus.

There are some who believe that Simon himself actually arranged for this woman to gatecrash his own feast, but I myself do not think there is a need to invent this idea. In Simon's mind, Jesus was living up to what he, Simon, thought of him in the first place—a dishonorable artisan who had no right to be telling others how to live honorably.

But Jesus was a prophet and therefore did read Simon's mind. But he didn't need to, actually. He knew what Simon had been up to in inviting him to a feast with those who deemed themselves Jesus' superiors. Jesus confronted Simon with a poser about two debtors who owed different amounts to the same creditor.

We need to remember that this was not like today, when you can decide to arrange a loan to pay for a car or a house. In those times peasants and peasant farmers were forced into debt to their landlords because of the rapacity of the landlords. Often small landowning farmers were forced to sell their farms and become tenant farmers, getting even further into debt in order to survive. Debt was not a voluntary arrangement, but the result of structural greed. And Simon knew this.

When Jesus asked which debtor would love his creditor the more when both debts were canceled, Simon answered, "The one, I suppose, to whom he forgave more." Simon, you see, could not imagine any debtor loving his creditor, since it was the creditor who caused the debt in the first place.

It was, in fact, a trick question from Jesus. Love is not the response of someone forced into debt by a creditor's greed and rapacity. Simon knew that the decision to cancel the debt made sound economic sense. It guaranteed the loyalty of the debtor, and, since the creditor owned the farm, it was better to cut his losses and let the debtor work harder to make sure there was no further need to get into debt again.

But Jesus had an important point to make, "Her sins, which are many, are forgiven, for she loved much; but he who is forgiven little, loves little."

Jesus, you see, turned his clever question around, making the point that love, not greed, can beget forgiveness. Because she showed Jesus such love and concern, the prostitute's sins—her debts to a rather different kind of creditor, God—are forgiven. This is not the case where God as a harsh and greedy creditor forces people into debt and then out of some selfish concern for the divine reputation, cancels the debt. This is the elder brother welcoming a loving but rejected member of the community into the surrogate family of God and placing her on an equal footing with all the other members of his family by canceling her sins—her debts to God and the community. Her love for Jesus and her desire to serve him moved him to cancel her debts.

He then formally makes public what had already happened between them, and says "Your sins are forgiven. Your faith in me and in God has brought you wholeness; go in peace." Notice, he does not say to her, "Go, and sin no more," as he had done to the woman taken in adultery. That woman had a choice about the way she lived: the prostitute did not. Jesus knew that she had no alternative but to continue in her prostitution unless she could find some family to adopt her. The surrogate family of God had to wait until after Jesus' resurrection and ascension before the family members shared their goods and thus prevented widows and other single women being enslaved in prostitution.

Simon's scheme to embarrass Jesus did not succeed. Instead, his own attitudes were shown up, and he was forced to learn the lesson that his wealth and position did not entitle him to play with the feelings and sensitivities of others. The prostitute learned that love and commitment from the heart bring their own reward, irrespective of a woman's place in society and her trade.

I have gone into more detail here because we can learn much from this narrative. We can reflect on the way we play the status stakes and how we sometimes make fun of those we see as either above us or below us. We can see here something of the redemptive power of selfless love and commitment to others, and to God.

I wonder if any of us can match the love and commitment to Jesus shown by this wonderful prostitute.

The Women who Acted as Patrons

> Soon afterward he went on through cities and villages, preaching and bringing the good news of the kingdom of God. And the twelve were with him, and also some women who had been healed of evil spirits and infirmities: Mary, called Magdalene, from whom seven demons had gone out, and Joanna, the wife of Chuza, Herod's steward, and Susanna, and many others, who provided for them out of their means. (Lk. 8:1–3 and Mat. 27:55–56; Mk.15:40–41)

Luke mentions that several women accompanied Jesus and the twelve on some of their missions throughout Galilee, and "ministered to them out of their means"—to render the Greek more accurately.

In Jewish society of that time this was a very outrageous thing for women to do. This was more than just cooking and serving meals. If a band of itinerant men needed someone to cook for them, then it would have been a male slave. The idea of a group of women going around with these men and ministering to them was unheard of. Where did they sleep at night? Did they journey separately from the men? Why were they not at home looking after their own menfolk? Women who traveled for other reasons than shopping and visiting relatives were always regarded with suspicion.

Luke says of them all that they were women "who had been healed of evil spirits and infirmities." This means that their response to the healing Jesus brought into their lives was to provide for him and the twelve out of their own means. Thus, Jesus and his disciples did not need to beg food and accommodation as they journeyed.

Luke names three of these women: Mary from Magdala, out of whom Jesus had cast seven demons; Joanna wife of Chuza, King Herod's steward; Susanna.

In this society, as in the Greco-Roman world of the time, women were never named in their own right. You will look in vain for the names of women in honorary inscriptions without also finding them named as the wife of, or the daughter of, or the sister of, or the mother of, some male person. The only exceptions were widows of extremely famous and powerful people.

It is important, then, to realize that when in the gospels a woman is named without reference to a male sponsor, then such a woman is a woman of shame. Mary of Magdala was shameful because of her demon-possession; Susanna is unknown, but because she was either sick or demon-possessed she would have been regarded as shameful. Joanna's sponsor is named: Chuza, a powerful member of the royal household of King Herod. She was the only honorable woman named in that trio. But by leaving her husband and journeying with this band of men she was bringing dishonor to her husband. We are not told how he handled that, but my guess is he found life in Herod's court rather difficult!

That Jesus accepted the personal ministrations of women

who were regarded as shameful says a great deal about his attitude to the customs of his days. But that they dared to be so public in their sponsorship of Jesus in the face of public outrage says something about their determination to respond to Jesus as women in their own right.

If a woman was seen as an object of shame, then her husband or father or son was never named in association with her, since this would extend the shame to him. Similarly, if a woman was named as being demon-possessed, her husband was never named.

It is also worth remembering that two of those women were chosen to be the first witnesses to the Risen Christ.

So we find a significant number of women who stepped right outside their social position and demanded to serve Jesus in their own way. In each case Jesus not only approved of their actions, but praised them.

It is also interesting to notice that most of these women served in ways that men refused.

4. Called to Serve

The First Witnesses to the Resurrection of Jesus

But on the first day of the week, at early dawn, they went to the tomb, taking the spices which they had prepared. And they found the stone rolled away from the tomb, but when they went in they did not find the body. While they were perplexed about this, behold, two men stood by them in dazzling apparel; and as they were frightened and bowed their faces to the ground, the men said to them, "Why do you seek the living among the dead? Remember how he told you, while he was still in Galilee, that the Son of man must be delivered into the hands of sinful men, and be crucified, and on the third day rise." And they remembered his words,

> and returning from the tomb they told all this to the eleven and to all the rest. Now it was Mary Magdalene and Joanna and Mary the mother of James and the other women with them who told this to the apostles; but these words seemed to them an idle tale, and they did not believe them. (Lk. 24:1–11 and Mat. 28:1–8; Mk. 16:1–8; Jn. 20:1–2)

In those days the word of a woman in a law court was never trusted. Her testimony had to be validated by at least two suitable males. You must also bear in mind that it is not too many years ago, in my lifetime, that the word of a pregnant woman could not be used on its own in the law courts of many western countries.

The women who go to the tomb to complete the task of embalming the body of Jesus are a motley lot; the Magdalene, the mother of James, Salome, Joanna and a few others who had been attending Jesus from the beginning of the movement in Galilee, and who had done what the male disciples refused to do: keep Jesus company during his crucifixion. An interesting and disparate group: one who had co-habited with seven demons, two who were wives of fishing entrepreneurs and honored in their village, the wife of a top official in Herod's household, and others with sufficient money to hire servants to do their household chores while they wandered with Jesus and the twelve.

The other interesting thing about this group of women is that none of them is related by blood to Jesus. The task of embalming was normally the responsibility of the blood relatives of the deceased. Where were Jesus' mother and his sisters? It seems that the women who went to the tomb regarded themselves as members of the surrogate family that Jesus had talked about—the family that had God as father and himself as elder brother, with all others as his siblings.

For all their money and dedication to the Messiah, they did not qualify in the eyes of the men who ran their society to be official witnesses to the most important phenomenon in human history—the resurrection of Jesus. Yet God chose them to be the first bearers of this momentous event, making God the most outrageous God in human history.

You would have thought that God knew better than that. You would have thought that God would have chosen to use the most respectable, trustworthy, honorable and socially acceptable people—men—to be the official heralds of the message that "He is risen!"

But no! Our outrageous God chose women, and these women were outrageous enough to accept this task without question and expect that they would be believed when they told the men this most unlikely of all truths: "Jesus is alive and will meet you in Galilee."

In John's Gospel, of course, they are not believed until Peter and John check the grave for themselves, thus fulfilling the requirement that two males validate a woman's testimony. Luke says of the men: "These words seemed to them an idle tale, and they did not believe them."

When Paul gives the list of those people to whom Jesus first revealed himself, you will notice a significant omission:

> For I delivered to you as of first importance what I also received, that Christ died for our sins in accordance with the scriptures, that he was buried, that he was raised on the third day in accordance with the scriptures, and that he appeared to Cephas, then to the twelve. Then he appeared to more than five hundred brethren at one time, most of whom are still alive, though some have fallen asleep. Then he appeared to James, then to all the apostles. Last of all, as to one untimely born, he appeared also to me. (1 Cor. 15:3–8)

All the gospels indicate that women were the first people to see Jesus alive and hear his voice. Here is Paul reporting what he had been told by Peter and James, that is, that they had been the first.

I wonder how Mary and her companions would have felt if they had been handed a copy of Paul's letter to the Corinthians?

Outrageous women will usually be put down by the men, especially in the church.

When God called upon women to serve with Jesus, God was taking a risk that the work of Jesus would be disregarded and dishonored in a society that placed little value on the word and work of women outside the household. Yet these same women were staunch and loyal followers of Jesus, standing beside him at the crucifixion when all but one of the men had run off in fear. Without the selfless devotion and commitment of these women, the actual work of Jesus and the twelve would have been much more difficult, for they made it possible for the men to give all their time to the proclamation of the kingdom without having to spend time and energy to organize food and accommodation.

5. Specially Chosen

This next group of women were specially chosen to make unique contributions to the work of God in the world—work that was almost indispensable. When seen from the perspective of the first century of our era, these women were being called upon to take a place well outside the one prescribed for them by men.

Elizabeth

> After these days his wife Elizabeth conceived, and for five months she hid herself, saying, "Thus the Lord has done to me in the days when he looked on me, to take away my reproach among men."

In those days Mary arose and went with haste into the hill country, to a city of Judah, and she entered the house of Zechariah and greeted Elizabeth. And when Elizabeth heard the greeting of Mary, the babe leaped in her womb; and Elizabeth was filled with the Holy Spirit and she exclaimed with a loud cry, "Blessed are you among women, and blessed is the fruit of your womb! And why is this granted me, that the mother of my Lord should come to me? For behold, when the voice of your greeting came to my ears, the babe in my womb leaped for joy. And blessed is she who believed that there would be a fulfillment of what was spoken to her from the Lord."

And on the eighth day they came to circumcize the child; and they would have named him Zechariah after his father, but his mother said, "Not so; he shall be called John." And they said to her, "None of your kindred is called by this name." And they made signs to his father, inquiring what he would have him called. And he asked for a writing tablet, and wrote, "His name is John." And they all marveled. (Lk. 1:24–25, 39–45, 59–63)

We first meet Elizabeth, mother-to-be of John the Baptizer, in Luke 1:5-7. She is described as the wife of Zechariah, who was a priest of the division of Abijah. She herself was from a priestly family, it being quite common for Jewish priests to seek out suitable wives from priestly families. She and her husband were "righteous before God, walking in all the commandments and ordinances of the Lord blameless."

But, she was barren and past the period of her fertility.

We need to remember that a woman's primary role was to give birth to children for her husband. This was an important part of her maintaining the honor of her husband's name in the family and village. Heirless husbands were objects of shame and reproach, while barren wives had no hope at all of ever being accepted in the community. The story of the treatment of Hannah in 1 Samuel 1:5–8 is typical.

Until a wife bore her husband a son, her position as a blood relative in the family was never secure.

The second-century *Book of James* provides an interesting insight into just how strong this bias was. Joachim had the right to be the first to offer his gifts to the Lord, but was prevented from doing so because he had no children. After searching the records he found that he was the only one in his tribe over several generations to be childless. He was so ashamed that he went out into the wilderness and fasted.[1]

Elizabeth, then, was seen as a source of her husband's loss of honor in his community, even though he carried out an honorable profession—the priesthood. The pressure laid upon Zechariah to take a young wife and raise up at least one son would have been enormous. However, he remained true to his commitment to Elizabeth, but prayed constantly for a solution to the problem of his loss of honor.

Since it was the man who suffered the dishonor, it was to the man that God sent the angel Gabriel with the assurance that God would resolve Zechariah's problem. His wife would conceive in her old age and have a son, who would take up a most important role: that of being the new Elijah to prepare Israel for the coming of the Messiah.

When she became pregnant in fulfilment of the angel's words, Elizabeth hid herself from public gaze by staying indoors for two good reasons: to make sure that no-one could accuse her of sexual misdemeanor by having intercourse with some young man; and to wait until she was so obviously pregnant that no-one could accuse her of lying.

During the sixth month of her pregnancy she was visited by her relative, Mary, the mother-to-be of Jesus. No sooner are the customary greetings over than Elizabeth's fetus makes an uncharacteristic movement inside her. The conversation between Elizabeth and Mary was typical women's talk of the day, always done behind closed doors. The fact that Luke was given access to some of the details means that he may have had some special relationship with Mary, for none of this is reported in the other gospels.

Elizabeth's response to Mary's news is one of joy for her kinswoman. She does not bemoan her own life of barrenness up to this time, but shares in Mary's delight at having her first child at such a young age. She also feels a special privilege at being chosen as the only one to be told of Mary's coming pregnancy.

Her great shout of praise, "Blessed are you among women, and blessed is the fruit of your womb!" has become enshrined in christian liturgy and prayer down the ages.

We need to be aware constantly that women's beliefs and any outbursts of praise and prophecy were not valued in that society. That these have persisted in the tradition and scriptures is to be seen as unusual and at risk of being decried by men.

In due time Elizabeth gave birth to her son and announced that his name is John, not Zechariah or whatever Zechariah's father's name may have been. Such naming caused consternation in the whole community, since the names of male children were important matters of the way families were bonded together. The father was required to assent to the name as a guarantee that he accepts that this child is his own. The giving of a name not included in the family networks was highly suspicious, and could lead to the suggestion that perhaps Zechariah was not the father.

But Zechariah, still dumb from the action of Gabriel because of Zechariah's doubts, is called upon to name his son. He does so in writing and confirms the name, John. Immediately he regains his speech and praises God.

The reaction of the community was predictable. The whole of the hill country in which Zechariah lived was buzzing for weeks. That a woman well past her fertile period should give birth was awesome enough—reminiscent of Abraham's wife, Sarah. But the name given to the baby,

69

John—"God has been gracious"—means that in some way he will not be embedded in the family. And that was proved to be the case when John left home to take up his residence in the wilderness, not to follow his father's profession of priest, but to be the second Elijah and announce the coming of the Messiah and the need of all people to prepare themselves for this coming.

Elizabeth fades from view from here onwards. She is now, at long last and in her old age, fully accepted as a wife and mother. All those years of shame and heartbreak are ended. Her husband has been restored to his honorable position as head of a household that has a son.

Her faithfulness in the midst of such community pressures is something we take too little account of. It is no wonder that God chose her—for she certainly proved God right!

Mary the Mother of Jesus

So little was known of this Mary that a family had to be invented for her in the second century. Thus, the Protevangelion of James says that her mother was Anna of Bethlehem and her father Joachim of Nazareth. We know of one sister from John 19:25, where this sister is among the women who stand by the cross of Jesus.

It would seem that she was from the house and lineage of David, sharing that tribal identity with her betrothed, Joseph.

It is something worth pondering on that God should choose for the mother of the Messiah a young woman whose father is not named and whose family tree is not outlined. It is even more amazing to remember that Matthew and Luke both proudly list the lineage of David, right back to Adam, when it was not to be Joseph's sperm that would help in the procreation process!

What we have here is the usual emphasis on the male head of the house with whom all the household is identified. His genealogy provided not only the identity but the honor, into which his wife, children and household slaves were embedded. Provided that the wife did not come from a foreign family or was not a slave, her genealogy was not so critical.

> In the sixth month the angel Gabriel was sent from God to a city of Galilee named Nazareth, to a virgin betrothed to a man whose name was Joseph, of the house of David; and the virgin's name was Mary. And he came to her and said, "Hail, O favored one, the Lord is with you!" But she was greatly troubled at the saying, and considered in her mind what sort of greeting this might be. And the angel said to her, "Do not be afraid, Mary, for you have found favor with God. And behold, you will conceive in your womb and bear a son, and you shall call his name Jesus.
>
> "He will be great, and will be called the Son of the Most High; and the Lord God will give to him the throne of his father David, and he will reign over the house of Jacob for ever; and of his kingdom there will be no end."
>
> And Mary said to the angel, "How shall this be, since I have no husband?" And the angel said to her,
>
> "The Holy Spirit will come upon you,
> and the power of the Most High will overshadow you;
> therefore the child to be born will be called holy,
> the Son of God.
>
> "And behold, your kinswoman Elizabeth in her old age has also conceived a son; and this is the sixth month with her who was called barren. For with God nothing will be impossible." And Mary said, "Behold, I am the handmaid of the Lord; let it be to me according to your word." And the angel departed from her. (Lk.1:26–38)

71

Here, God's angel goes directly to the woman, not to her husband or betrothed, as in the case of Elizabeth. This is in itself unusual. Once Mary had been betrothed to Joseph, she was embedded in him and his family, with him as her sponsor.

Betrothal was a much more public ceremony than in the west today. The match between the groom and bride was formally conducted in a public ceremony in the village square. Both family heads would have been involved in lengthy negotiations involving the dowry and the living arrangements for the bride. The contract was usually arranged by the two fathers, with the mothers having significant input. The contract was announced and signed on a well-advertized day in the midst of the villagers.

The only delay for the couple was the time it would take to arrange the wedding ceremony. The important point is that they were in fact married by the exchange of contracts at the betrothal ceremony, but did not live together until the actual wedding ceremony. Until then, the bride-to-be was not available for social gatherings and had to behave as though she was already a wife. Should any man have intercourse with her, that would be an act of adultery and they could both be stoned. If the husband-to-be wanted to pull out of the betrothal, then he had to get a bill of divorce.

Thus, when Gabriel came to Mary, she was already "married" to Joseph. All communication should have been addressed to him and not to her. This is one reason, no doubt, why Matthew, who is much more careful to show that his central characters kept the social niceties, omits the visit of Gabriel to Mary, but has the angel visit Joseph to assure him that Mary's pregnancy was not the result of an adulterous act, but caused by the direct intervention of God's Holy Spirit.

Thus, Mary had two good reasons to be troubled by Gabriel's visit. The first was that he came to her and not to Joseph. How on earth would she ever be able to tell Joseph about this? There were no male witnesses to this visitation. The second reason was the greeting given her by Gabriel: "Rejoice! O one on whom God has been pleased to endow grace! The Lord be with you!"

Mary, being the modest and humble woman that she was, was deeply troubled by this greeting. Why was not her betrothed husband thus greeted? She had no status or honor apart from him. Gabriel reassures her and gives her the prophecy that her son is to be the Messiah and ruler over the future house of David. But how can this possibly be? She has not been publicly married and therefore cannot have intercourse with Joseph. Indeed, she is not allowed to mix with any male company until the village wedding.

Gabriel then explains what is to happen to her. God's Holy Spirit will cause her to become pregnant in a way that will ensure the child will be male and will be "holy": that is, dedicated to the service of God. It is important to remember here that "holiness" describes the space and purpose, not the inner quality. This baby, Jesus, is to be dedicated to the service of God—indeed will be, by act of God, the son of God.

What Mary is being told is that God will assume the traditional role of husband in her case: God will make her a mother, and will protect her.

It is as though Mary is being given the news that God is going to set up a surrogate family to replace the family of Israel; God will be the father, she the mother and Jesus the elder brother. All subsequent children she bears to Joseph will be junior to Jesus.

This notion of the surrogate family is to be the model that the early christians will use to explain their movement.

Mary's response is simple, but honest. She cannot really comprehend what it all means, but she says to Gabriel, "Behold I am the slave of God; let it be to me according to your word."

The English word "handmaid" (which we are used to) is far too weak. She calls herself a female slave, the one that waits on her master and does his every bidding without question, without pay and without any redress. A slave has no rights to family and kinship, no rights to personal possessions and no will. Hers is an unquestioning and absolute response of submission to the God who sent Gabriel with this message.

She is reassured by the knowledge given her by Gabriel

73

that her relative Elizabeth is already six months pregnant, in spite of her age. As with Elizabeth, Mary's son is named ahead of time by God. This would have been perceived to confer a great deal of honor on the child when born. In both cases, the name is not from the genealogy, thus signifying a special holiness for each boy.

After recovering from what must have been a rather traumatic experience for her, Mary goes off to see her cousin Elizabeth. Notice, she does not go and see Joseph. They are not supposed to mix socially, unless others are present, until the wedding day. And who would believe this fantastic story of the visitation by Gabriel and the message she had been given? Certainly none of her friends and family would ever believe that God would choose to speak to her and not first to Joseph.

I have already dealt with the meeting between Mary and Elizabeth, so I want to concentrate on the prophecy that Mary uttered.

> And Mary said,
>   "My soul magnifies the Lord,
> and my spirit rejoices in God my Savior,
> for he has regarded the low estate of his handmaiden.
>   For behold, henceforth all generations will call me blessed;
> for he who is mighty has done great things for me,
>   and holy is his name.
> And his mercy is on those who fear him
>   from generation to generation.
> He has shown strength with his arm,
>   he has scattered the proud in the imagination of their hearts,
> he has put down the mighty from their thrones,
>   and exalted those of low degree;
> he has filled the hungry with good things,
>   and the rich he has sent empty away.
> He has helped his servant Israel,
>   in remembrance of his mercy,
> as he spoke to our fathers,

74

> to Abraham and to his posterity for ever."
> And Mary remained with her about three months, and
> returned to her home. (Lk. 1:46–56)

Let me offer the following translation in order to counter our over-familiarity with the words we use so often in our liturgies. I am trying to let this young Mediterranean woman speak to us in her own words.

> With my mind I exalt the Lord,
> and with my whole inner being I exult in God my redeemer,
> because God has taken note of my slavelike subservience.
> You will see that from now on all generations will declare
> that God has treated me as special,
> because the Powerful One has done mighty things for me.
> Holy be God's Name,
> and divine mercy continue from generation after generation
> to the ones making obeisance to the Powerful One.
> With an arm the Lord creates sovereignty
> and puts to route the arrogant in the conceit of their hearts.
> The Powerful One has dethroned authorities
> but has promoted subservients;
> the starving ones God has satiated with good
> and the self-satisfied dismissed empty.
> God has been fully devoted to Israel the beloved one
> as a memorial to divine mercy;
> just as was said to our ancestors,
> to Abraham and to his descendants for ever.

No translation from one language to another can ever fully reflect all that is going on in the text and in the speaker. But I hope that this translation will cause you to think again about words you have probably read and sung many, many times.

75

Mary, having been honored by the angel Gabriel in a way that she cannot believe she has deserved, pours out her heart, not only in heartfelt thanks to God for choosing her for such an honored position as the mother of the Messiah, but in a burst of pent-up hope for the revolution that her selection may bring about.

Male oral poetry was usually a rather formal, public affair—the putting together of familiar sayings from the Psalms and the prophets. You have only to read the outburst of Zechariah in the temple at the circumcision of his son to see that. It is full of the usual hopes and prayers that occur in each act of worship.

But women's oral poetry, which was usually said in private when women got together for their socializing and bonding, was much more likely to be revolutionary—going into subjects that women were not supposed to even think about, let alone sing about.

Mary's song—and she would have sung it to a familiar chant—is just full of topics women would never discuss in front of their menfolk. She is characterizing the God of Israel as one who has directly chosen a woman to take part in the founding of the new Israel. She has suggested that the God of Israel has mercy on all people, not just on Israel. She has described God as overturning the economic and social structures of Jewish society. She has claimed that all this revolutionary activity by God was in fact all there in the promises made to Abraham, Isaac and Jacob.

Had Mary sung that song before her betrothed Joseph and in her village square, she would have been stoned for blasphemy!

Luke says that Mary stayed with Elizabeth for about three months before returning home. That means she left a day or two before the birth of John, helping her cousin Elizabeth during those last difficult weeks of pregnancy when she would need the kind of support that only a woman could give. Remember, Elizabeth had hidden herself when she became pregnant, so she would not have had anyone else to call on.

Luke does not tell us exactly when Mary conceived, but it could well have been soon after Gabriel's visit, so that her pregnancy would have become evident to both her and Elizabeth while she was there. We can see in these two women a great strength of purpose, and in Mary a particular sense of destiny for herself and the son in her womb. But this sense of destiny was to be sorely tried and she would stumble from time to time. After she had given birth to Jesus and the visitation of the shepherds, Luke writes that "she kept all these things, pondering them in her heart."

Luke gives us clues as to the social status of Joseph. The baby was dressed in swaddling clothes, usually thought of as the clothing of the poor. The practice of wrapping babies tightly to restrict their freedom was certainly a common one at the time, and still persists in some cultures. Joseph was an artisan, and would not have had the resources to clothe his son in expensive garments. It was only after the visit of the Magi with their costly gifts that there was any spare money available.

This Mediterranean virgin, who was burdened with a secret she could share only with her cousin Elizabeth, faced a difficult time ahead, with suspicions of adultery against her, and claims of illegitimacy against her son.

We see her next quietly presenting her son for circumcision and hearing the prophecies of Simeon and Anna. Every year at Passover, she and Joseph took him to the temple at Jerusalem. And then, when Jesus was twelve, was the special journey when he was to undergo the ritual of becoming a "son of the law." This marked his progress into puberty and the right to take some part in synagogue worship. It also marked his transition from the world of his mother to the world of his father. From this moment on, Joseph takes over as leading parent, with Mary now in the background.

The emotional attachment of the son to his mother will never disappear, and it will often be harder for the mother to give up the education and discipline of her son to her

77

husband. But, this is the way of the Mediterranean family, and both Jesus and Mary must conform.

> Now his parents went to Jerusalem every year at the feast of the Passover. And when he was twelve years old, they went up according to custom; and when the feast was ended, as they were returning, the boy Jesus stayed behind in Jerusalem. His parents did not know it, but supposing him to be in the company they went a day's journey, and they sought him among their kinsfolk and acquaintances; and when they did not find him, they returned to Jerusalem, seeking him. After three days they found him in the temple, sitting among the teachers, listening to them and asking them questions; and all who heard him were amazed at his understanding and his answers. And when they saw him they were astonished; and his mother said to him, "Son, why have you treated us so? Behold, your father and I have been looking for you anxiously." And he said to them, "How is it that you sought me? Did you not know that I must be in my Father's house?" And they did not understand the saying which he spoke to them. And he went down with them and came to Nazareth, and was obedient to them; and his mother kept all these things in her heart. (Lk. 2:41–51)

What is noticeable in this story is that, while Jesus has made the transition from the female world to the male world quite readily, Mary has not. When Jesus has been found to be missing and his parents return to Jerusalem and find him still in the temple, it is Mary and not Joseph who has the first word. "Son, why have you treated us so? Behold, your father and I have been looking for you anxiously." Mary should have left Joseph to handle this situation.

Jesus respectfully rebuked her for not knowing where he would be, showing a self-awareness about his new status as the son of his father.

Once again, Luke says that Mary kept all these things in her heart.

From here on, Mary surfaces rarely in the gospel narrative. Her son has taken up the trade of his father, as was expected. Once Joseph has died, Jesus takes over as head of the household. We know of two brothers and several sisters that Jesus would have been expected to care for. He was now the sponsor of his mother and sisters. Family honor demanded that he provide for them, and for his sisters he had to find suitable husbands and dowries. He would help his younger brothers set up their own households as they came of marriageable age.

When Jesus, aged thirty, walks out of that house to begin his messianic mission, he was perceived by his village and family to have acted dishonorably. Leaving his mother and sisters without a suitable sponsor was unpardonable; and there would be times when he would be reminded of that. I mention this here in a book about women because it is an important factor in understanding the behavior of Mary.

Mark shows Mary trying to get Jesus back into the house. He had been doing a great deal of healing of sickness and casting out of demons.

> Then he went home; and the crowd came together again, so that they could not even eat. And when his family heard it, they went out to seize him, for people were saying, "he is beside himself." And the scribes who came down from Jerusalem said, "He is possessed by Beelzebub, and by the prince of demons he casts out demons" ... And his mother and his brothers came; and standing outside they sent to him and called him. (Mk. 3:19–22, 31 also Mat. 12:46–50; Lk. 8:19–21)

79

Mary is still dealing with the dishonor Jesus has brought to her husband's name, and now he is accused of being insane—even possessed by the very demons he is casting out of other·people. She wants to get him inside the house and out of public view.

The only other time Mary comes into the narrative in her own right, apart from the crucifixion scene and being with the eleven after Jesus' resurrection, is at the wedding feast where Jesus turns the water into wine.

> On the third day there was a marriage at Cana in Galilee, and the mother of Jesus was there; Jesus also was invited to the marriage, with his disciples. When the wine failed, the mother of Jesus said to him, "They have no wine." And Jesus said to her, "O woman, what have you to do with me? My hour has not yet come." His mother said to the servants, "Do whatever he tells you." Now six stone jars were standing there, for the Jewish rites of purification, each holding twenty or thirty gallons. Jesus said to them, "Fill the jars with water." And they filled them up to the brim. He said to them, "Now draw some out, and take it to the steward of the feast." So they took it. When the steward of the feast tasted the water now become wine, and did not know where it came from (though the servants who had drawn the water knew), the steward of the feast called the bridegroom and said to him, "Every man serves the good wine first; and when men have drunk freely, then the poor wine; but you have kept the good wine until now." (Jn. 2:1–10)

A marriage is a village affair, where two families are bonded in public. The groom and bride are not the chief focus, but the two families. There have been months of negotiation, the public exchange of contracts and then the feast at which the two meet for the first time since the betrothal.

The fact that Mary is there with Jesus and the twelve disciples shows that they are close friends of the two families. This is made even more obvious when you realize that Mary was involved with the catering. The main feast was usually in the bride's parents' home, and was the main preliminary to the groom conducting the bride to his home for the consummation. But in this case it seems to have been held in the groom's parents' house. This means that Mary was probably a close relative of the groom's family.

A crisis looms as the wine supply dwindles to a danger-
ously low point. The honor of the groom's father is now
threatened. He has asserted the true status of his family and
possessions when bargaining with the bride's family about
the size of the dowry he expects from them. He has done his
best to provide a son that will keep his honorable position in
the community intact.

If the wine does run out, then the whole community—not
just those attending the feast—will accuse him of acting
above his status, pretending he has more money that he really
has. Going off to the nearest wine seller and trying to nego-
tiate more wine may even add to that, for the vintner will
seize the opportunity to double his prices!

Mary goes to her son with a plea that he do something to
save the situation. The honor of her friend's husband must be
saved.

Since her own husband is dead, Mary's status is embedded
in her son's. Although he has dishonored the family by leaving home and walking away from his responsibilities, she sees
an opportunity for Jesus to rehabilitate the family name. If she
can persuade him to save the day in some attention-getting
way, then the community may give her back her husband's
honor.

But Jesus, as always, is not inclined to become involved in
the honor-shame games of his community. His enigmatic
reply, as the Greek has it, "O woman, what (is it) to me and
to you? My hour is not yet" is telling Mary that what she
wants he cannot give in the way she longs for. She wants
some public affirmation of her son's power and position; he
will solve the problem without drawing attention to himself
at all.

Jesus' moment of supreme honor is death on the shameful
and dishonoring cross. He will do nothing to retrieve his
social status as perceived by his community. The miracle he

performs is seen only by the slaves who serve the guests with the wine. The comment of the chairman of the feast that this lot of wine is of superior quality is a further sadness for Mary. If only the whole gathering could know that it was her dishonorable son who had saved the occasion from disaster by changing water into this wonderful wine!

Mary needs to be seen as she really was—a true Mediterranean woman, embedded first in her husband and then in her son, finally handed on to the apostle John, to be embedded in his family until her death.

In many ways she acted outrageously in her early years; but, once Jesus began his mission, she was to be sorely tested as her expectations in terms of honor for her son and herself gradually faded. Sadly, we hear nothing from her after Jesus' resurrection, so we have no way of knowing how she reacted to the kingdom as it actually emerged. In true Mediterranean tradition, the men of the early church drew no attention to her whatsoever.

The Adulteress

Including the woman taken into adultery in the list of those especially chosen seems strange at first glance. But, whereas the first two were chosen by God to play important roles in the kingdom, this woman was chosen by Jesus' enemies to play what they expected would be a crucial role in dishonoring him. In the event, Jesus turned the tables on them and used her to make an important statement about the status of women in society.

> The scribes and the Pharisees brought a woman who had been caught in adultery, and placing her in the midst they said to him, "Teacher, this woman has been caught in the act of adultery. Now in the law Moses commanded us to stone such. What do you say about her?" This they said to test him, that they might have some charge to bring against

> him. Jesus bent down and wrote with his finger on the
> ground. And as they continued to ask him, he stood up and
> said to them, "Let him who is without sin among you be the
> first to throw a stone at her." And once more he bent down
> and wrote with his finger on the ground. But when they
> heard it, they went away, one by one, beginning with the
> eldest, and Jesus was left alone with the woman standing
> before him. Jesus looked up and said to her, "Woman,
> where are they? Has no-one condemned you?" She said,
> "No-one, Lord." And Jesus said, "Neither do I condemn
> you; go, and do not sin again." (Jn. 8:3–11)

Adultery was a sin against the husband. The wife, embedded in her husband, had no place at all outside his status. His honor was maintained by her sexual faithfulness to him, while any unfaithfulness brought him shame. Wives were expected to be virgins on marriage; any signs of a lack of virginity annulled the marriage. Any evidence of her sexual misconduct as a wife meant instant divorce. The husband had no choice in the matter. This was an open society—nothing happened behind closed doors that did not come out into the open fairly quickly. Privacy as a value was unknown.

This woman must have been married for a charge of adultery to be leveled, for a married man having sexual intercourse with a single woman was not adultery. She was chosen by Jesus' enemies to trick him into denying the validity of the Mosaic Law. No doubt his liberal attitude towards women had become well known, and these foes wanted to use this as a way of attacking him. If he said that she should not be stoned to death for her crime, then he could be brought before the temple authorities and charged with teaching others to break the law. If he agreed to her stoning, they would be able to take him before the Roman authorities and charge him with breaking their law, since it was illegal for Jews in Israel to carry out a death sentence without first getting the approval of the Roman governor.

Of course, their plot did not work because Jesus turned the tables on them by challenging their own law-keeping standards. "Let the one who has never broken a law throw the first stone." These men knew each other pretty well, and knew that not one of them had ever been a perfect lawkeeper. For any man there to have picked up a stone would have been to make a claim to honor that all the others knew to be false. He would have been jeered at.

They all realized they had been outmaneuvered and gradually dispersed, beginning with the oldest and most respected, for these had the most to lose: only the young and foolish might try to tough it out.

The woman was left alone with Jesus. She had made no protest. She had not asked, "Why did you not bring the man too? It takes two to commit adultery." She could have claimed that she had been set up by one of those present, for how else could she have been seen in the act? Her adulterous partner could well have been among the accusers.

Jesus asked her a rather obvious question, "Has none of these man laid a formal charge against you?"

Her simple reply of "No-one, sir" elicited Jesus' now famous words, "Neither do I lay any charge against you. Off you go and do not repeat the offense."

What is remarkable here is that Jesus does not question her to find out the truth. He accepts that she did commit the offense. But what is also remarkable is that, while Jesus does not condone this act of adultery, he does appear to suggest that divorce will not necessarily follow.

When asked about divorce in Mark's gospel, Jesus extends the grounds for divorce to a husband's unfaithfulness to his wife, thus giving married women the right to initiate divorce, a rather rare phenomenon in those days in Israel.[2]

This woman had been chosen by Jesus' enemies to be used against Jesus, but in the end was used against them.

Her meekness and acceptance of the shameful situation she found herself in, and her reluctance to try and extract herself from what was clearly an injustice, resulted in her being forgiven. Can there be any doubt that she would ever commit adultery again?

These three women were especially chosen as examples of the fact that God does not confine his prophetic word and call to a position of responsibility to men. Without the willing cooperation of women like these, even when it meant their going against the customs and even the law of their day, the world and the church would be in a much poorer state.

6. Self-Servers

There are always those who care only about themselves and nothing about anyone else. This is not confined to men. Indeed, the Old Testament is replete with women who behaved badly.

These two women, a mother and her daughter, are the only "bad" women named in the gospels. They belonged to the family of Herod, and had an unsavory reputation.

Herodias and her Daughter

For Herod had sent and seized John, and bound him in prison for the sake of Herodias, his brother Philip's wife; because he had married her. For John said to Herod, "It is not lawful for you to have your brother's wife." And Herodias had a grudge against him, and wanted to kill him. But she could not, for Herod feared John, knowing that he was a righteous and holy man, and kept him safe. When he heard him, he was much perplexed; and yet he heard him gladly. But an opportunity came when Herod on his birthday gave a banquet for his courtiers and officers and the leading men of Galilee. For when Herodias' daughter came in and danced, she pleased Herod and his guests; and the king said to the girl, "Ask me for whatever you wish, and I will grant it." And he vowed to her, "Whatever you ask me, I will give you, even half of my kingdom." And she went out, and said to her mother, "What shall I ask?" And she said, "The head of John the Baptizer." And she came in immediately with haste to the king, and asked, saying, "I want you to give me at once the head of John the Baptizer on a platter." And the king was exceedingly sorry; but because of his oaths and his guests he did not want to break his word to her. And immediately the king sent a soldier of the guard and gave orders to bring his head. He went and beheaded him in the prison, and brought his head on a platter, and gave it to the girl; and the girl gave it to her mother. When his disciples heard of it, they came and took his body, and laid it in a tomb. (Mk. 6:16–29 and Mat. 14:1–12)

We know from Josephus,[3] the Jewish historian of the first century of our era, that Herodias' daughter by her first husband, Philip, was called Salome.

Herod Antipas had been appointed tetrarch of Galilee in 4BC. Not content with the limited power that he, a son of Herod the Great, had been given, he demanded to be a client king of Caesar. For such temerity, he was deposed and banished in AD39. But while in power he seemed to arrogate to himself the title of king, which is why Mark calls him king.

Herodias was herself a granddaughter of Herod the Great and also half-niece of Herod Antipas. She married Philip, a son of Herod the Great, and Philip the tetrarch of the gospel story. It was her daughter Salome who was married to this Philip, who was her uncle. The whole Herodian family is riddled with incestuous relationships, so it is little wonder that their history becomes a little confused.

It seems that John the Baptizer publicly condemned Herod Antipas for divorcing his first wife, a Nabatean princess, in order to marry Herodias, also divorced from Herod Philip.

Such public revelations of the acts of the powerful elite would certainly have been strongly disapproved of, and the Baptizer was imprisoned, probably at the behest of Herodias, who stood to lose the most by his public revelations.

That Herod is afraid of John is an important marker of the respect and honor in which he was held by the people. It was this kind of fear and jealousy that was the eventual cause of Antipas' downfall. The public feast Herod organized to mark his own birthday was a typical act of honor maintenance. He did this because it was expected of him, not just because he was a generous and open-hearted ruler. Mark tells us who were invited: his court attendants, his army officers and the civic leaders of Galilee. So this was an important gathering of the elite of Galilee.

When Salome came in to dance, she did a shameful thing. Dancing by women was only ever done before family and kin. That honorable men at the top of the ruling elite allowed such a shameful thing to happen meant that they lost honor in the eyes of the rest of the community. This was further compounded by Herod allowing himself to become bewitched by the sensuousness of Salome's dancing. It becomes quite clear that all this was organized by the two women in order to extract something from Herod. Under normal circumstances he would never have allowed this to happen. When Herod in his besotted and no doubt drunken state offered her all she was entitled to receive as a woman, half his assets, she went straight to her mother. But this plot was not about money. It turned out to be a scheme to secure the execution of the hated Baptizer.

By having Herod make his pledge before all these honored guests, the women made certain that they had him trapped. There was no way he could crawl out from under. Had this happened at a private, family party, they might not have succeeded. Herod had to keep his pledge, no doubt glad in one

87

way at not losing half of his assets to a woman he could never have for his own while his wife—her mother—was still alive.

We can only gaze in disgust and dismay at the sight of the bleeding head of John the Baptizer, the last of the Hebrew prophets, sitting on a silver salver and being carried off in triumph by these two horrible women. Here were women who knew how to manipulate the games of honor and shame among men to serve their own evil desires.

7. Women in Jesus' Parables

In the three parables that follow, Jesus used women to give a positive lesson on behavior that went outside the one value that women were to exemplify: purity and virginity. Proverbs 31:10–31 gives us a typical picture of the "ideal woman" in the Mediterranean world. Her world is inside the home, industrious and managerial, allowing her husband to spend his time in drinking coffee with the other husbands in the village square.

But Jesus shows that women have far more to offer, even when some do not live up to their responsibilities.

The Ten Maidens

"Then the kingdom of heaven shall be compared to ten maidens who took their lamps and went to meet the bridegroom. Five of them were foolish, and five were wise. For when the foolish took their lamps, they took no oil with them; but the wise took flasks of oil with their lamps. As the bridegroom was delayed, they all slumbered and slept. But at midnight there was a cry, 'Behold, the bridegroom! Come out to meet him.' Then all those maidens rose and trimmed their lamps. And the foolish said to the wise, 'Give us some of your oil, for our lamps are going out.' But the wise replied, 'Perhaps there will not be enough for us and for you; go rather to the dealers and buy for yourselves.' And while they went to buy, the bridegroom came, and

> those who were ready went in with him to the marriage feast; and the door was shut. Afterward the other maidens came also, saying, 'Lord, lord, open to us.' But he replied, 'Truly, I say to you, I do not know you.' Watch therefore, for you know neither the day nor the hour. (Mat. 25:1–13)

A wedding was a great social occasion for the whole village. The two families being united are extremely careful about making sure that everything in the ceremonies and feasting reflects their social position.

This is a ten-bridesmaid wedding. That makes it a very important occasion for the super elite of the village. While everyone will be able to come out and watch the activities, only the elites have been invited to the feast and formal occasions.

The particular part of the ceremony that Jesus uses for his parable is that moment when the groom leaves his parents' house to go to the bride's parents' place to conduct her to the place that will be his and his bride's. This house was usually within a stone's throw of his parents' house.

You will notice that the Jews at some stage changed from the Genesis tradition (where the groom goes to live with his bride's family) to the tradition here where the bride is re-embedded in her husband's family.

The groom leaves for his bride's parents' house and at this point the ten bridesmaids join the procession to the groom's house. Here, all the official guests are already reclining and feasting, waiting for the couple to join them. At the end of the feast the groom will conduct his bride to the bedroom, and consummate the marriage. He will then return to the feasters and display the bloodstained sheet that attests to his masculinity and to his bride's virginity. This will be greeted with cheers and acclamations.

The honor of both sets of parents is very much at stake here. (It is also interesting to note that this custom still prevails in many Mediterranean communities to this day.)

In the parable, the groom delayed at his parents' house. Mothers the world over are always loath to give up their sons; while fathers typically want to make sure that all the financial arrangements are in order. Whatever the reasons, the groom arrived late at his bride's house. All the ten bridesmaids had fallen asleep, the excitement of the occasion taking its toll. Their lamps had been lit to light up the entrance to the bride's parents house, but five of the lamps had gone out and there is no more oil to relight them. The five girls try to persuade the others to share the remaining oil with them. But to no effect, for if the groom delays too long, then all the lamps will go out, and then where will the procession be!

So, it's off to the nearest oil supplier to wake him up in the dead of night and beg some oil from him. The fact that such merchants were at home and not at the wedding indicates just how high up on the social scale were the people involved in this wedding. By the time they returned, the groom had arrived and taken his bride to his house.

The effect of their carelessness was to reduce the wedding from a ten-bridesmaid ceremony to a five-bridesmaid one, thus bringing dishonor to the groom's family, by whom they had been chosen. Not only had all these young virgins been carefully selected to make sure they belonged to the blood lines of both families, but their mothers would have spent days training them in the dances and songs they had to perform, and in making sure they knew how to dress and how to look after their lamps.

Their lack of attention to one matter—the amount of oil to take in order to account of any unusual delay on the part of the groom—led to the spoiling of the whole occasion.

In the parable Jesus calls them by a very terrible word. "Foolish" in English goes nowhere near the intensity of the meaning. "Moron" is the closest we can come. He calls them "morons"; they had no excuse whatsoever, since they had been properly trained and instructed for their role. They had brought shame to the whole occasion. The entire village would have felt insulted. It would be years before the people of that village could hold up their heads before neighboring villagers who would never cease to remind them of this disaster.

But, notice, it is not the wise virgins who are used as the main point of the parable. They did what they were trained and expected to do, so there is no praise for them. Doing one's duty brings no rewards!

The morons in the parable are used by Jesus to make the point about the coming kingdom of God. When the groom shut the door after entering his new house, he was doing a most unusual thing. In those days doors were not shut on feasts: they were deliberately kept open in order to show that the honorable status of the participants had been more than maintained.

So why was the door shut for this feast? Passers-by and gapers would soon take note of the place of the missing bridesmaids. The shame they brought had to be shut off from public gaze. The bloodstained sheet would be displayed only to the official guests and not to the whole village. So great, you see, was the social effect of the one mistake these morons of bridesmaids had created. This was not a matter of ignorance: they had been told exactly what to do. This was a mistake made out of stupidity and lack of attention to detail.

Thus Jesus used two kinds of women to make important points. Doing exactly what you are prepared for and in the way expected of you brings no acclamation. Duty is done because it is expected. You need to exceed your duty to win any praise and honor, and that was almost impossible in Mediterranean society.

Also, doing your social duties ensured that the good order of your community would continue in peace and harmony.

Duties and traditions were important to the Mediterranean world, far more important than laws, for they played a much more critical role in the maintenance of peace and prosperity.

The one failure of the five moronic virgins caused havoc in the whole community, not just in the wedding ceremony. Dishonor and shame were brought to the two families, and disruption to the life of the whole village.

Jesus' summary of the parable, "Watch therefore, for you know neither the day nor the hour," could be put like this: "See that you pay attention to even the slightest and least important detail of your life, for a failure in even the smallest detail will affect the good of everyone else in your community."

We are so individualistic in the way we live our lives, relate to each other and serve God, that this aspect of Jesus' parable escapes us.

Thus, Jesus uses two kinds of women to tell us very important things about our witness and service to God; and in doing so sets them outside their normal sphere—the home—to make his points.

The Woman who Lost a Coin

> "Or what woman, having ten silver coins, if she loses one coin, does not light a lamp and sweep the house and seek diligently until she finds it? And when she has found it, she calls together her friends and neighbors, saying, 'Rejoice with me, for I have found the coin which I had lost.' Just so, I tell you, there is joy before the angels of God over one sinner who repents." (Lk. 15:8–10)

In this parable, Jesus sets the woman where she is expected to be—in her home. Unlike the setting of the previous parable, here we have a poor woman. Her dowry was just ten drachmas—ten days wages of a worker. She had to look after her dowry for her husband, who was not allowed to spend it. It would be used to hand on to the husband of his eldest daughter. The dowry symbolized the social status of this family, and the whole village would have known how large or small it was.

She probably had the coins sewed into a kerchief, to be worn around her head on important days so that her husband's honor could be displayed. To lose one was a disaster. So she sweeps the house from top to bottom, using up oil during the day to light her lamp so she can see into the dark corners where the coin could have rolled, until she finds it and sews it back into its place.

She then calls in her neighbors and friends and, as women would then have done, goes through the whole saga: showing them which coin had gone missing, how she had lit the lamp and swept the whole house out, and then showing them exactly where she found the coin. And notice, she admits to having lost the coin.

This is the kind of bonding that women do so well, and ensures the continuation of the social fabric of the community.

Men, of course, only celebrate their successes and good deeds: failures are never talked about. In the parable that precedes this one in Luke, there is a rich landowner who lost one of his hundred sheep. He leaves the ninety-nine in the care of his dogs and goes off and finds the lost one. When he returns he celebrates with his neighbors but you will notice that he does not accept any blame for the sheep being lost.[4]

The honesty of this woman and her readiness to admit her faults before her friends is thus set in sharp contrast to the dishonesty of men in claiming only their successes and never admitting to their faults in public.

Jesus leaves no doubt as to which kind of person will find a welcome in heaven.

The Widow who Challenged a Judge

> And he told them a parable, to the effect that they ought
> always to pray and not lose heart. He said, "In a certain city
> there was a judge who neither feared God nor regarded
> man; and there was a widow in that city who kept coming
> to him and saying, 'Vindicate me against my adversary.' For
> a while he refused; but afterward he said to himself,
> 'Though I neither fear God nor regard man, yet because
> this widow bothers me, I will vindicate her, or she will wear
> me out by her continual coming.'" And the Lord said, "Hear
> what the unrighteous judge says. And will not God vindi-
> cate his elect, who cry to him day and night? Will he delay
> long over them? I tell you, he will vindicate them speedily.
> Nevertheless, when the Son of Man comes, will he find faith
> on earth?" (Lk. 18:1–8)

Widows in Hebrew society, like orphans, were totally vul-
nerable, as I have already shown. They were not able to
inherit their late husband's estate or earn any income (other
than in the street). They had no male to speak for them in the
public courts or assemblies.

Thus, widows become the symbol of the powerless, voice-
less and oppressed.

In this parable, the judge is described as being shameless:
he has no sense of the difference between what is sacred—
belonging to God—and what is profane—what belongs to
the people. For such a judge, the letter of the law is all that
matters, no matter what the cost.

The widow had a legal problem and with no man to go to
court on her behalf, she was powerless and would lose out to
her adversary. So she decided to go to his home and speak
directly to him. This was outrageous in the extreme. She had
no right to take such action, and any move on his part to
even take notice of her would have brought him into great
disrepute.

But she stuck to her plan and made herself so obnoxious

to him that he had no option but to take notice of her. Once having done that, he must stick to the letter of the law and decide in her favor. Her outrageousness in going outside the bounds of her position in society brought its reward.

Jesus goes on to point out that God is not like that judge. God does take immediate notice of all those who appeal for justice and vindicates them. And, whereas the judge in the end was shamed into action by the persistence of the widow, God is honored by the speedy vindication of the oppressed.

Thus, three groups of women are used by Jesus in parables to show the kind of standard that is expected of all believers. In choosing women, Jesus himself was being quite outrageous in an era when women were valued only as adjuncts to men.

I now move on to those women who figure in the Acts of the Apostles to see whether the same trends continue in the life of the early church.

Notes

1. Protevangelion of James 1.2–4, *New Testament Apocrypha* ed. Hennecke and Schneemelcher.
2. Mk. 10:2–12
3. Antiquities of the Jews 18.5
4. Lk. 15:4–7

PART 3

Women in the Acts of the Apostles

Introduction

There were quite a few women who featured in the life and leadership of the first generation of christians. I want to introduce them and show just how significant their contribution was.

The first mention of women in Acts occurs immediately after the ascension of Jesus. The eleven disciples return to the upper room in Jerusalem where they "devoted themselves to prayer, together with the [i.e. some] women and Mary the mother of Jesus, and with his brothers."[1]

This is the only mention of Jesus' mother outside the gospels. According to John's gospel, Mary had been taken out of her family and given over to the care and sponsorship of the apostle John,[2] thus taking away the responsibility for caring for her from Jesus' brother James. It is significant that Luke separates Mary from Jesus' brothers, thus supporting John's account. The natural way of referring to them would have been something like "together with Jesus' brothers and his mother, Mary."

It is important to remember that women were always identified in terms of their relationship to a male, whether husband, brother, son, uncle or cousin. A woman with no male relative to act as her sponsor was an embarrassment in this ancient society.

What is significant here, though, is that these women joined with the eleven apostles in prayer. This was unheard of in early Judaism, where women were invariably segregated from the men in the synagogues. That they took an active part in the prayer life of the early church was quite outrageous behavior and was, in fact, to become a sore point with Paul in Corinth.

When Peter later addressed the large meeting on the day of Pentecost, he addressed the men only.[3] This was because he was talking to Jews. The three thousand souls added to the church that day would have included the women and children of those men baptized. Luke specifies that women were being added to the Lord as well as men.[4]

The Widows of the Hellenists

> Now in these days when the disciples were increasing in number, the Hellenists murmured against the Hebrews because their widows were neglected in the daily distribution. And the twelve summoned the body of the disciples and said, "It is not right that we should give up preaching the word of God to serve tables. Therefore, brethren, pick out from among you seven men of good repute, full of the Spirit and of wisdom, whom we may appoint to this duty. But we will devote ourselves to prayer and to the ministry of the word." And what they said pleased the whole multitude, and they chose Stephen, a man full of faith and of the Holy Spirit, and Philip, and Prochorus, and Nicanor, and Timon, and Parmenas, and Nicolaus, a proselyte of Antioch. These they set before the apostles, and they prayed and laid their hands upon them. (Acts 6:1–6)

Sadly, language has been a great divider of people ever since God destroyed the human lust for divinity at the Tower of Babel. Among the early disciples of Jesus were those who spoke mostly Hebrew and those who spoke mostly Greek. The Hebrew-speaking disciples, led by Peter, seemed to have assumed that they were superior and that those women who had no male sponsors to care for them—called generally "widows"—who were Hebrew-speakers should have the lioness's' share of the common fund.

Peter, of course, was not prepared to arbitrate on this. So he opted out by suggesting that the Greek-speakers should appoint seven men from their number to make sure that the Greek-speaking widows would be properly cared for. What you see happening here is these seven men becoming the joint sponsors of these women, making sure that they were adequately fed and clothed and housed. Here we see the separation of gospel preaching and social work, a trend that would continue until women forced a change.

What is important in this story is that these Greek-speaking widows no doubt made themselves heard and attracted the attention of the men to do something about the injustice and cultural prejudice that was disadvantaging them. In doing that they went far beyond what society generally allowed them.

It is interesting to notice that the care of widows was the very first social service project undertaken by the fledgling church. But, why widows? Because, as I have pointed out, such women with no extended family to take care of them were reduced to begging and often prostitution. Male orphans could find work, but not female orphans or widows.

This was the beginning of a whole new attitude where people were helped on the basis of their need rather than on the basis of maintaining the honor of the donors. As these women were to be fed and clothed and housed from resources provided by the common pool, there was no way that anyone's name was to be associated with this work.

It is noteworthy that when Paul started his persecution of the church, "He dragged off men and women and committed them to prison."[5] He would not have bothered with women unless he felt they were a powerful force in the early church.

Sapphira

> But a man named Ananias with his wife Sapphira sold a piece of property, and with his wife's knowledge he kept back some of the proceeds, and brought only a part and laid it at the apostles' feet. But Peter said, "Ananias, why has Satan filled your heart to lie to the Holy Spirit and to keep back part of the proceeds of the land? While it remained unsold, did it not remain your own? And after it was sold, was it not at your disposal? How is it that you have contrived this deed in your heart? You have not lied to men but to God." When Ananias heard these words, he fell down and died. And great fear came upon all who heard of it. The young men rose and wrapped him up and carried him out and buried him. After an interval of about three hours his wife came in, not knowing what had happened. And Peter said to her, "Tell me whether you sold the land for so much." And she said, "Yes, for so much." But Peter said to her, "How is it that you have agreed together to tempt the Spirit of the Lord? Hark, the feet of those that have buried your husband are at the door, and they will carry you out." Immediately she fell down at his feet and died. When the young men came in they found her dead, and they carried her out and buried her beside her husband. And great fear came upon the whole church, and upon all who heard of these things. (Acts 5:1–11)

What was outrageous about Sapphira was that she wanted to act as an equal partner with her husband, Ananias. And in that she was accepted by Peter. But it entailed accepting her share of the responsibility of the pretense that the total proceeds of the sale of their land had been given to the common pool.

What was at stake in this incident was that Ananias and Sapphira wanted to have both the reciprocal honor of the outside community and the recognition of the christian community for having given up a piece of land for the sake of those in need.

As land owners, they would have been required to give money to their local synagogue for the payment of scripture scrolls, furniture and scribes' stipends. In return their names would have been recorded as being attached to such gifts. Once they gave their assets away, they would have no more money with which to continue maintaining their honor in this way, and that would attract the sneers of their neighbors. This was why they planned to retain some of the proceeds of the sale, to continue to make their usual benefactions to the community and to be honored and respected in return.

The problem with giving to the common congregational pool—laying the proceeds at the feet of the apostles—was that the donors' names became detached from particular gifts. There was also the situation that the gifts made from the common pool were based upon the need of the recipients for help and not on the perceived need for the donors to be honored. Since the recipients needed the money for basic sustenance they were in no financial position to respond by writing up the names of the donors—even if they knew them—on synagogue walls or on the notice boards of public buildings.

Thus Ananias and Sapphira wanted the continued respect of their community for publicly recognized benefactions, and at the same time to be known by the christian community as having given up their saleable assets for the support of the widows, orphans and anyone else in need. But, since there was only word-of-mouth recognition on the occasion of the donation, with no way of knowing who had received any of their money, Ananias and Sapphira—as with all those who gave their assets to the apostles—would not get any permanent public recognition for this.

The two were condemned for preferring the public honors of their community to the knowledge that their gift had

101

saved a number of fellow believers from penury. This led them to pretend that what they had laid at the feet of the apostles was the total proceeds of the sale of their land.

In coming separately to the apostles to record her part in the donation, Sapphira was acting outside her role as wife. She was wanting a separate recognition for her part in the donation rather than allowing her husband to take all the credit, as he was entitled to do in her society.

Having arrogated to herself such a status, she was also entitled to be judged separately. Thus Sapphira paid the price of selfishly stepping outside her social position and of trying to hold onto her status in the community while pretending to be selflessly caring for the needy in her christian community.

Mary the Mother of John Mark

> When he realized this, he went to the house of Mary, the mother of John whose other name was Mark, where many were gathered together and were praying. And when he knocked at the door of the gateway, a maid named Rhoda came to answer. Recognizing Peter's voice, in her joy she did not open the gate but ran in and told that Peter was standing at the gate. They said to her, "You are mad." But she insisted that it was so. They said, "It is his angel!" But Peter continued knocking; and when they opened, they saw him and were amazed. But motioning to them with his hand to be silent, he described to them how the Lord had brought him out of the prison. And he said, "Tell this to James and to the brethren." Then he departed and went to another place. (Acts 12:12–17)

After Peter had been imprisoned by Herod, following the popularity Herod gained with the Jewish authorities after murdering James, brother of John, some of the disciples met for prayer in the house of Mary, mother of John Mark.

This Mary is notable for two things: the first because she did not sell her house, give the proceeds to the twelve for the care of the poor and live off this charity; and second because she allowed her house to be used for christian worship. She is the only person named as having her house used in this way. While in Rome, Corinth and other Roman cities outside Jerusalem there was no immediate danger in doing this, in Jerusalem this was very dangerous. The christians had to give up meeting in the temple and the synagogues because of the persecution they suffered. Luke tells us that there were some eight thousand converts and that there was a steady increase in this number.

Where did these people meet, if not in the homes of those with large enough areas to accommodate more than an average family?

Mary's decision to keep her home and use it in this way was in fact a rather courageous one, risking both the ire of the Jewish authorities and the criticism of other believers who thought she should have sold it and shared her wealth with them.

Mary had a slavegirl named Rhoda. That she continued to keep her as a slave and not manumit her is significant, but it is obvious she had begun to treat her as a human being. It was not until Paul enunciated the principle of deferring to each other that the institution of slavery in the Roman empire began to be undermined, taking several centuries to disappear.

Rhoda

When he realized this, he went to the house of Mary, the mother of John whose other name was Mark, where many were gathered together and were praying. And when he knocked at the door of the gateway, a maid named Rhoda came to answer. Recognizing Peter's voice, in her joy she did not open the gate but ran in and told that Peter was standing at the gate. They said to her, "You are mad." But she insisted that it was so. They said, "It is his angel!" But Peter continued knocking; and when they opened, they

> saw him and were amazed. But motioning to them with his hand to be silent, he described to them how the Lord had brought him out of the prison. And he said, "Tell this to James and to the brethren." Then he departed and went to another place. (Acts 12:12–17)

It is important to understand that Rhoda was a slave, not a paid housemaid or servant. She was a slave. Most translators have been reluctant to use this word because of the implication that Mary, mother of John Mark and a believer, owned one or more slaves.

The institution of slavery was absolutely necessary for the stability of the economy of the Roman empire. Without slavery, the empire would have collapsed. The Hebrews continued to own slaves, as several of Jesus' parables indicate. Paul had things to say to christian slave-owners to make them realize that one aspect of slavery—that a slave was an object to be possessed and not a person to be related to—must not apply to them.

Peter had been imprisoned for no specific crime by Herod Antipas, who had recently executed James, the brother of John. When Herod found that the Jewish temple bureaucracy really appreciated this disposal of the leader of the hateful christians, he decided to capitalize on that and do the same with Peter, by then quite well known around the temple and the city. But Peter was released from prison by an angel of the Lord. So he went to where he knew some of the leaders were praying for him—the house of Mary.

When Rhoda was faced at the door with a Peter no longer in prison, she didn't stop to close the peep hole and open the door to let him in, but rushed off and shouted to all those gathered for prayer that Peter was out of prison.

This gives us a clue that Mary was already treating her slavegirl as a human being. In other circumstances, Rhoda would have walked quietly up to her mistress and whispered the news to her. But, of course, being the word of a woman, and a slave into the bargain, her joyous outburst was not believed, and so it was some minutes before those men took notice of Peter's continued knocking and shouting and went to let him in.

Thus Rhoda joins those women whose words were not believed because of her sex. But that did not stop her from telling her story and sticking to it, and being proved correct.

Tabitha

> Now there was at Joppa a disciple named Tabitha, which means Dorcas. She was full of good works and acts of charity. In those days she fell sick and died; and when they had washed her, they laid her in an upper room. Since Lydda was near Joppa, the disciples, hearing that Peter was there, sent two men to him entreating him, "Please come to us without delay." So Peter rose and went with them. And when he had come, they took him to the upper room. All the widows stood beside him weeping, and showing tunics and other garments which Dorcas made while she was with them. But Peter put them all outside and knelt down and prayed; then turning to the body he said, "Tabitha, rise." And she opened her eyes, and when she saw Peter she sat up. And he gave her his hand and lifted her up. Then calling the saints and widows he presented her alive. And it became known throughout all Joppa, and many believed in the Lord. And he stayed in Joppa for many days with one Simon, a tanner. (Acts 9:36–43)

The management of finance and the organization of charity were always in the hands of men in that patriarchal society. It was some time before women were allowed to become equal with men in the practical service of the christian congregations.

When we read that Tabitha "was full of good works and doing acts of mercy," we need to understand that in this she was stepping outside what was considered to be the role of women in the congregations. What she was doing was rather different from those women in the gospels who accompanied Jesus and arranged food and accommodation for him and the twelve during their wanderings in Galilee. Tabitha was doing what so far only men had been commissioned to do: look after widows.

There is no indication as to why she did this work. We know from the next chapter that there was another disciple there, a man named Simon, a tanner; for it was on his roof that Peter had the vision that led him to Caesarea and Cornelius the centurion.

There can be no doubt, though, that the reason Peter brought Tabitha back to life was for the sake of the widows that she took care of, and not for her sake.

Tabitha was the forerunner of many women who were to take their place in the congregations as carers of the widows and orphans, a role normally expected of men then.

Lydia

Setting sail therefore from Troas, we made a direct voyage to Samothrace, and the following day to Neapolis, and from there to Philippi, which is the leading city of the district of Macedonia, and a Roman colony. We remained in this city some days; and on the sabbath day we went outside the gate to the riverside, where we supposed there was a place of prayer; and we sat down and spoke to the women who had come together. One who heard us was a woman named Lydia, from the city of Thyatira, a seller of purple goods, who was a worshiper of God. The Lord opened her heart to give heed to what was said by Paul. And when she was baptized, with her household, she besought us, saying, "If you have judged me to be faithful to the Lord, come to my house and stay." And she prevailed upon us. (Acts 16:11–15)

It is often forgotten that the Jewish synagogue was basically an organization of men: women were allowed in but had to worship separately. When, in Philippi, Lydia led a group of women to meet for prayer down by the river, she did that because what they were doing was technically not allowed to Jewish women without the leadership of men. The riverside was where women went to do the family washing, so there was hardly any likelihood of being seen by men.

There must have been very few Jewish household heads in Philippi. If there had been at least ten Jewish adult males, they would have been required to meet as a synagogue for worship. It seems that no such synagogue meeting was happening in Philippi.

But Lydia was not Jewish. She had become attached to a Jewish synagogue in Thyatira in Asia Minor as a "worshiper of God"—the term used for non-Jews who attached themselves to a synagogue without actually converting to Judaism. As a gentile woman who had no male sponsor—she was a single businesswoman—conversion was not available to her anyway. As there were probably a number of Jewish women among this group, she led them down to the women's laundry by the river on sabbath days to join with some of the gentile women she had encouraged to worship the Jewish God with her.

When Paul and Silas arrived and sat down with them and began to teach them about Jesus being the Messiah, she and the others stayed. This was an unusual situation for those days, as women were not usually thought of as the recipients of philosophy or religious teaching, especially in Judaism.

When she accepted Jesus as her Messiah, she called for her household slaves to join her in christian baptism. That in itself was not unusual, for Luke has already written about the way the centurion Cornelius called for his family and slaves to join him in baptism under Peter. But it is Lydia's next reaction that is really outrageous: she turns to Paul and says to him, "If you have judged me to be faithful to the Lord, come to my house and stay." Luke re-inforces the unusual nature of this request by adding, "And she *prevailed* upon us." The verb here has connotations of asking for something that is not according to custom or law.

As a single, unattached woman, Lydia was in a difficult position socially. She was a businesswoman and had plenty of money. She may have taken over the business from her husband after he died in war or a shipping tragedy. Inviting three single men to live in her house was not a socially acceptable thing for her to do. But she wanted to make some appropriate response to these men who had acted outside social custom by sitting down with her and her women friends and teaching them about the Messiah. This no doubt emboldened her to be equally outrageous and offer them accommodation for some days.

I believe that Lydia was to be a salutary lesson to Paul, forcing him to re-examine his own patriarchal attitude to women. It is also interesting that Paul's acceptance and encouragement of women in both Philippi and Thessalonica are often in sharp contrast to his attitude to women in Corinth and other cities. When Paul and Silas ran into trouble a little later in Thessalonica they had the support of "not a few of the leading women."

I have no doubt that Paul had a great deal to thank the outrageous Lydia for during a rather stressful time in Macedonia.

Damaris

> But some men joined him and believed, among them Dionysius the Areopagite and a woman named Damaris and others with them. (Acts 17:34)

Paul had found Athens, centre of Greek life and culture, very unsettling. He was disturbed by the abundance of shrines and statues to Greek and Roman divinities that lined the streets of the city. As he tried to proclaim Christ as the son of the only true God in the marketplace, he kept coming up against pagan philosophers who laughed at him.

Word of this Jew with a new philosophy about Jesus and Anastasia—*anastasia* is the Greek word for resurrection, but Paul's superstitious listeners immediately took it to be the name of some new god—reached the ears of those whose responsibility it was to make sure that all the philosophers who set up their schools in the city had been properly vetted. So they called upon Paul to give a guest lecture at their council meeting.

Paul tried very hard to get through to these highly educated but superstitious people. He used some of their own well-known philosophers and poets to show that he was simply building on what had already been taught. But when they finally found that "anastasia" was not the name of a new god but referred to the resurrection of Jesus, they cut him off before he had time to finish, promising to hear him at another time.

However several people who were there did become believers. Luke names only two: Dionysius the Areopagite (who must have been one of the members of the council) and a woman named Damaris. Her name is a variant of "heifer" and suggests she was a high-class prostitute, especially since the only women who were allowed to attend the theater and meetings such as Paul had just addressed were courtesans. This would explain why Luke does not name her father or any male sponsor, since to do so would have shamed them because of her profession. It would have taken a great deal of courage on her part to become a believer, especially as she may have been rather well known, which was why Luke named her.

We never hear more of Damaris, and we do not hear anything about Athens again, either. It seems that Athens was not to play any significant part in the formation of the early church. Indeed it was some centuries before Athens would provide any significant christian leadership at all.

Prisca

> After this he left Athens and went to Corinth. And he found a Jew named Aquila, a native of Pontus, lately come from Italy with his wife Priscilla, because Claudius had commanded all the Jews to leave Rome. And he went to see them; and because he was of the same trade he stayed with them, and they worked, for by trade they were tentmakers. (Acts 18:1–3)

> After this Paul stayed many days longer, and then took leave of the brethren and sailed for Syria, and with him Priscilla and Aquila. (Acts 18:18)

> He began to speak boldly in the synagogue; but when Priscilla and Aquila heard him, they took him and expounded to him the way of God more accurately. (Acts 18:26)

Luke draws attention to two Jews from Rome, Aquila and Priscilla, a husband-and-wife team of tent-makers who had been among those expelled from Rome. They had set up a tent-making business at Corinth, where Paul joined them as a fellow-craftsman. It was probably there that they became believers.

When Luke next mentions them, he calls them "Priscilla and Aquila." Luke uses the diminutive form of her correct name, "Prisca." By putting her name first, Luke is saying something about her development in the faith. He does the same thing when he has them arrive in Ephesus and teach Apollos the full christian faith. For a woman to be involved in teaching a man, and a missionary into the bargain, was indeed outrageous! Luke was risking the ire of his readers by naming her first.

The Four Unmarried Daughters of Philip

> On the morrow we departed and came to Caesarea; and we entered the house of Philip the evangelist, who was one of the seven, and stayed with him. And he had four unmarried daughters, who prophesied. (Acts 21:8–9)

Philip was one of the seven elected by the Greek-speaking disciples among the Jerusalem congregations to look after the daily distribution to the Greek-speaking widows.[6] After the murder of Stephen he had gone into Samaria and won many to the Lord.[7] He was then sent by the Spirit towards Gaza where he baptized the Ethiopian eunuch.[8] From thence he went to Caesarea, where he must have married and settled down.[9]

For a man to have one unmarried daughter was considered an embarrassment; but to have four was unheard of! What was wrong with them that no husbands could be found for them?

The author of Acts tells us what their problem was: they were prophets.

I have already pointed out when citing the case of Anna[10] that women were not welcome as prophets. But Paul had already had some experience with women exercising a prophetic ministry at Corinth.[11] Thus, while Philip would not have been honored in the general Caesarean community because of his four unmarried daughters, he was quite comfortable with having them exercise their prophetic ministry in the congregation that probably worshiped in his home.

It is easy for us to miss the force of Luke's comment on these daughters. Since he has identified Philip as one of the seven, why the necessity of mentioning the daughters unless there was something unusual about them? From the perspective of Theophilus, to whom Acts was addressed, the unmarried daughters needed to be accounted for in order to preserve the honor of their father.

111

Paul's Sister

This is the only mention of any member of the family of Paul of Tarsus (Acts 23:16). In this case it is his nephew who is credited with overhearing the plot to kill Paul as he was being transported from Jerusalem to Caesarea by the Roman authorities. Neither sister nor nephew is named, even though Luke must have known them through his close relationship with Paul.

Who Paul's father was or how many siblings he had is never mentioned. All that can be deduced from this passage is that his sister was married and that her son remained loyal to Paul, even though Paul had become a leading member of that group of Jews who had accepted Jesus as their Messiah and had thus earned the hatred of the leaders of the Jewish temple in Jerusalem. It could well have been that after Paul's encounter with the risen Christ on the Damascus road and during the fourteen or so years he stayed in Tarsus, he persuaded his whole family to accept Jesus as Messiah.

The only other women named in Acts are two prominent women in the Roman administration.

Drusilla

She is named as the wife of Felix, procurator of Judea. She was in fact his third wife. Antonius Felix was himself a freedman, probably manumitted by Antonia, mother of the emperor Claudius. All we know of Drusilla is that she was the daughter of Herod Agrippa I.

Bernice

She was the sister of Herod Agrippa II, governor of the whole region that included Caesarea, and was the elder daughter of Herod Agrippa I, who gave her in marriage to his brother Herod Philip. After her husband's death, she lived in her brother's house in a relationship that was claimed to be incestuous. She later married Polemon, king of Cilicia, the region in which Paul's city of Tarsus lay, but soon left him to return to her brother.

You can have some idea of what Paul's feelings were towards her when he saw her attend his trial before her brother Agrippa (Acts 25:13).

It can be seen that women played a very important part in the life of the early christian church. Not only were they starting to take on some of the responsibilities for social work which were normally the domain of men, but they started to make their presence felt at the leadership level.

As I will show, this was to lead to some tensions as the church moved out into the Roman world, but it did not stop women from assuming responsibility under God for the day-to-day operations of the christian congregations of which they felt they were equal members.

Notes

1. Acts 1:14
2. Jn. 19:26–7
3. Acts 2:14
4. Acts 5:14
5. Acts 8:3
6. Acts 6:5
7. Acts 8:4–13
8. Acts 8:26–39
9. Acts 8:40
10. pp. 30–2
11. 1 Cor. 11:5

Women in Paul's Epistles

When you look at the people named in the epistles of the New Testament, you find there is a surprising number of women. This is unusual enough in itself, but, unless a married couple is being referred to, all these women are named in their own right, and not as being under the sponsorship of some male. This would have been quite unacceptable to both the Jewish and Graeco-Roman society of the time.

What we are seeing here is the admittance of women into the world of males, and an acknowledgment that God has seen fit to override the social prejudices of the day.

Romans 16

The very first in a long list of people at Rome that Paul greets personally is

> . . . our sister Phoebe, deacon of the church at Cenchreae, that you may receive her in the Lord as befits the saints, and help her in whatever she may require of you, for she has been a benefactor of many and of myself as well. (Rom. 16:1–2)

Phoebe may have delivered Paul's letter to the Roman church herself. This was unusual, and was probably because of her being a rich benefactor in her own right at Cenchreae. Paul has no hesitation in breaking with custom and demanding that she be treated according to her position in the community and not according to her sex. She joins those wealthy women who supported Jesus and his disciples with their money.

There is no evidence in the New Testament itself for an exact description of the role and function of a deacon. But what is certain is that Phoebe is the only deacon who is named. She must have given outstanding service to the church at large to have become the only deacon named in the whole of the early church.

The fact that Paul chose to name her as a deacon is a very strong indication of the important part being played in the leadership of the early congregations by women.

There is a very interesting inscription from the fourth century of our era, found at Jerusalem:

> Here lies the slave and bride of Christ, Sophia, deacon, the second Phoibe, who fell asleep in peace on the 21st month of March during the 11th indiction . . . the Lord God . . .[1]

Here is a fourth-century woman deacon being likened to first-century Phoebe; both are deacons and both are rich benefactors of the Christian community. This shows just how unusual Phoebe must have been in her day to have been remembered three hundred years later.

Prisca is greeted next. Paul always uses her proper name, not the diminutive Priscilla, and places her ahead of her husband, Aquila, thus showing his great respect for her. He refers to the fact that she and her husband "risked their necks for my life, to whom not only I but also all the churches of the Gentiles give thanks" (Rom. 16:3–5).

They now have a house church meeting in their Roman home, so they are back there after the expulsion order on the Jews had been repealed. They were also to establish a house church at Ephesus, where they had a great influence on the missionary Apollos.

Mary is noted as one who "worked hard among you" (Rom. 16:6). In this, she is being accorded the same status as any of the men who worked hard in Rome.

It is worth noting here that gospel work, whether evangelism or building up congregations, was described as "manual labor," for this is the word for "work" that Paul consistently uses. In fact, most of the references to "work" in Paul's letters are about gospel work and not manual labor.

Mary is thus one of the many women who worked side by side with Paul and his male coworkers in proclaiming the gospel of Christ. Their work was as exhausting and as crucial as the men's.

Junia is probably the wife of Andronicus. They are described as "my kinsmen and fellow prisoners, people of note among the apostles, and they were in Christ before me" (Rom. 16:7). Junia is thus senior in the faith to Paul, something that Paul would be possibly rather reluctant to admit! The fact that he does ascribe Junia seniority in the faith is really a quite outstanding thing for a man like Paul, who was brought up from childhood to believe that women's place was in the home under the patronage of their father.

Paul does not name Junia as the wife of Andronicus and this is important, for it shows that Paul accepted her in her own right and not just as the wife of Andronicus.

117

Tryphaena and **Tryphosa** are two women who are described also as "workers in the Lord" (Rom. 16:12). They could well have been sisters, even twins, as it was not unusual to give twins similar-sounding names. Tryphaena is also the name of a fictitious queen of Pisidian Antioch who showed kindness to Thecla in *The Acts of Paul*, a second-century romance.

Julia is probably the wife of Philologus (Rom. 16:15). Her name suggests a connection with Caesar's household.

The sister of Nereus is greeted. Nereus was a close friend of Flavia Domitilla, a christian lady of the Roman imperial family, who was banished to the island of Pandateria by her uncle Domitian in AD95.

Thus, of those 28 greeted by name, eight are women—some 29%. This shows just how much Paul valued the work and leadership of women; and that despite the cultural sanctions against women playing leadership roles in either civic or religious life.

1 Corinthians

Chloe is named as the source of Paul's claim that there is much quarreling among the believers at Corinth (1 Cor. 1:11). The term "Chloe's people" suggests that she was the leader of a house church there or at Ephesus, from where Paul was writing. This is very important, for it means that she may also have led the worship, even presiding at the Lord's Supper.

Prisca is mentioned again, this time as having a house church in Ephesus and sending greetings with her husband Aquila to the believers at Corinth (1 Cor. 16:19).

Philippians

Euodia and **Syntyche** are described as having "labored side by side with me in the gospel together with Clemens and the rest of my fellow workers, whose names are in the book of life" (Phil. 4:2–3). They are thus on equal footing with all those men who worked with Paul at Philippi. Too often the disagreements between these two women are emphasized rather than the fact that they are accorded equal status with the men in the work of the gospel there. Their names are also in "the book of life," so Paul does not seem to want to waste too much energy on resolving their problems. His main concern is that the work of the gospel in which they are all involved is not damaged in any way by the disagreements between them.

Colossians

Nympha is the head of a house church at Laodicea (Col. 4:15). She is another woman who probably presided at the Lord's Supper.

2 Timothy

Paul reminds Timothy that both his grandmother **Lois** and his mother **Eunice** were in Christ before him. It is significant that neither the grandfather nor father rates a mention (2 Tim. 1:5). Even if they were not believers, the fact that they are not named is significant, since women were always named as the daughter, sister, wife or mother of some male.

An even more significant point is that Timothy's father was a Greek and not a Jew (Acts 16:1). According to Jewish tradition, Timothy was a Jew through his mother, which was why Paul insisted on circumcising him when he asked Timothy to join in his mission. Paul did not want Jews to use Timothy as proof that Paul was opposed to the law of Moses.

What is important here is that the Jewish tradition was being passed on to Timothy through his mother and grandmother; and when they became Christians through Paul, they continued Timothy's education in the gospel. In this, they risked the anger of the Greek community and of Timothy's father, since it was expected that Timothy would follow his father's profession, whatever that was.

What is significant here is that these two women were responsible for teaching the faith to a male. In this they went right outside the norms of both their culture and their husbands'. A mother traditionally took no further part in the rearing of any male children once they reached puberty and became the responsibility of the father.

Yet Timothy is reminded to take careful note of what these two women had taught him after he became a christian, which would have happened in his adulthood.

These were two strong women of solid convictions who were prepared to be shamed by their local Greek community in order to make sure that Timothy continued steadfast in their newfound faith in Christ.

Prisca is again greeted (2 Tim. 4:19), as is **Claudia** (2 Tim. 4:21).

Philemon

Apphia is greeted as "our sister" and is a member of the house church of Philemon (Philem. 2).

It is interesting to note that Paul refers to Apphia as "our sister," while the others named are called "fellow workers," "fellow soldiers" and "fellow prisoners."

Paul often makes a distinction between those who worked with him in his mission and those who were members of established congregations. In this case, Apphia is a member of the congregation that meets in the home of Philemon.

We have here an example of the church as the surrogate family of God, with Jesus as the elder brother and everyone else his siblings. No distinction is being made between the male and female siblings for purposes of social status and leadership. It seems that in the early stages of the church, leadership was "gender neutral," to use a term of today.

These are all the women greeted or mentioned by name in the New Testament.

What comes through loud and clear is that in the early church women were included as equals within the leadership and ministering of the congregations and missionary activities. Women are named as individuals in their own right, only being mentioned in association with a man when the husband is being included. This in itself was radical enough, let alone that women are shown as teachers, dispensers of charity and leaders of house churches. If the order of deacon is what is meant by the word "diakonos," then one woman, Phoebe, is the only deacon named.

The respect thus shown to women served to set the early church apart, not only from its own secular community, but from the church from the second century onwards.

Notes
1. *New Documents Illustrating Early Christianity* Vol. 4 p.239.

Paul's Comments on Women

Whenever Paul comments on women in general and makes statements about their place in the congregations, we must always take into account the special circumstances and the context of the city and region involved. Too often what Paul has said about women in a particular place has been universalized, as though Paul meant his words to apply to all women in all places for all time. A careful study of the problems Paul faced in each of these cities will show quite clearly that what he says about women and their place in the life and work of the church was dictated by the particular circumstances he found in the church there. Often the power of the worship of a pagan goddess dictated the way women were looked upon in a region; this makes it even more important to take such things into consideration before quoting Paul's comments about women in a particular place and applying them uncritically and generally.

At Corinth

This Roman city had a worldwide reputation for its sexual licentiousness. The worship of Aphrodite was exceptionally strong at Corinth, resulting in temple prostitution. There were also a great number of street prostitutes, whose quarters can still be seen today among the Roman ruins. Sailors were keen to disembark at the two seaports of Corinth and sample the street girls.

It was also the case that women generally were denigrated there. Not one example of a woman in public office has come down to us from the early Roman period.

Bearing in mind that the christians met in small groups in the homes of the wealthy, and that many of the women converts would have been ex-prostitutes, you must have some sympathy with Paul and his reluctance to bring the gospel into disrepute—as he saw it—by having ex-prostitutes praying and testifying. But it was also a fact that women generally were disparaged in Corinth, so that their taking part in congregational worship and teaching would have been inappropriate in Paul's mind.

It is the general attitude of the Corinthian men to women, as well as the renown of Corinth as the acme for the sex tourists of the day, that should be borne in mind when reading what Paul had to say about Corinthian women. We must note that he did not say these things about women in any other city.

> The body is not meant for immorality, but for the Lord, and the Lord for the body. And God raised the Lord and will also raise us up by his power. Do you not know that your bodies are members of Christ? Shall I therefore take the members of Christ and make them members of a prostitute? Never! Do you not know that he who joins himself to a prostitute becomes one body with her? For, as it is written, "The two shall become one flesh." But he who is united to the Lord becomes one spirit with him. Shun immorality. Every other sin which a man commits is outside the body; but the immoral man sins against his own body. Do you not know that your body is a temple of the Holy Spirit within you, which you have from God? You are not your own; you were bought with a price. So glorify God in your body. (1 Cor. 6:13–20)

Paul wrote this in answer to questions being asked by members of the congregations at Corinth. Unfortunately for us,

Paul does not repeat the question, so we have to try and work out exactly what he was actually being asked.

Bearing in mind that unmarried men were very much in the minority in the ancient world, what we have here is a question about the use of street prostitutes by married men. But what is strange about Paul's answer is that he treats it as a religious issue and not a moral issue. He could so easily have invoked the seventh commandment, even though strictly speaking the married man would not be committing adultery unless the prostitute was married, for adultery was a sin against the married man, not the woman. However, he would have been told about Jesus' restatement of the law, making it adultery if a married man had intercourse with an unmarried woman. The Jews among the christian leaders in Jerusalem were very concerned about the lax morality of the gentile world, and so would have been careful to tell Paul about what Jesus had said. But he certainly could have appealed to the various christian sanctions against sexual promiscuity.

Instead, Paul treats this as a religious problem.

What is known is that the street prostitutes of Corinth looked to Aphrodite as their patron, even if they did not serve as temple prostitutes. To such a prostitute, having sex with a stranger was in some way an act of service to Aphrodite.

Paul is saying, then, that when a christian man, who believes that Christ's Spirit inhabits his body, is united with a prostitute who believes that the spirit of Aphrodite inhabits her body, the overall mystical effect is that Christ is having sex with Aphrodite. He emphasizes this by pointing out, referring to the second chapter of Genesis, that sexual intercourse is not just a pleasurable experience, like eating; but is an act that joins the man and the woman in a spiritual way.

Our western notions of individuality and love-based sex were almost unknown in the Roman world. Marriage for "love" and commitment was rare. Marriage was a social

125

institution for the procreation of children and the regulation of women. For a Roman man to have sex with a prostitute was not seen as threatening the institution of marriage. He would have seen that as his right; but would, at the same time, instantly divorce his wife should she have sex with anyone else.

Thus, in this passage, Paul is not being harsh on women as women. Indeed, he is according them a right to have their own experiences. The problem, as he saw it, was that these prostitutes believed that they were serving Aphrodite and at the moment of intercourse were representing her, giving the man the experience of mating with the god. No matter that the men could claim that, as christians, they knew that the pagan gods had no objective existence and so Aphrodite did not exist and thus they were having sex only with the prostitute.

Paul is more concerned with the perceptions of the non-christian prostitute and the effect it would have on her and how she would then perceive christian men who continued to use prostitutes. He would also be concerned for those prostitutes who became christians and how they would feel when they saw male members of their congregation resorting to prostitutes.

In Paul's view, each believer's body was a temple of Holy Spirit, and that temple should not be polluted by introducing pagan presences into it.

Now concerning the matters about which you wrote. It is well for a man not to touch a woman. But because of the temptation to immorality, each man should have his own wife and each woman her own husband. The husband should give to his wife her conjugal rights, and likewise the wife to her husband. For the wife does not rule over her own body, but the husband does; likewise the husband does not rule over his own body, but the wife does. Do not refuse one another except perhaps by agreement for a season, that you may devote yourselves to prayer; but then come together again, lest Satan tempt you through lack of self-control. I say this by way of concession, not of command. I wish that all were as I myself am. But each has his own special gift from God, one of one kind and one of another.

To the unmarried and the widows I say that it is well for them to remain single as I do. But if they cannot exercise self-control, they should marry. For it is better to marry than to be aflame with passion.

To the married I give charge, not I but the Lord, that the wife should not separate from her husband (but if she does, let her remain single or else be reconciled to her husband)—and that the husband should not divorce his wife.

To the rest I say, not the Lord, that if any brother has a wife who is an unbeliever, and she consents to live with him, he should not divorce her. If any woman has a husband who is an unbeliever, and he consents to live with her, she should not divorce him. For the unbelieving husband is consecrated through his wife, and the unbelieving wife is consecrated through her husband. Otherwise, your children would be unclean, but as it is they are holy. But if the unbelieving partner desires to separate, let it be so; in such a case the brother or sister is not bound. For God has called us to peace. Wife, how do you know whether you will save your husband? Husband, how do you know whether you will save your wife?

Only, let every one lead the life which the Lord has assigned to him, and in which God has called him. This is my rule in all the churches. Was any one at the time of his call already circumcised? Let him not seek to remove the marks of circumcision. Was any one at the time of his call uncircumcised? Let him not seek circumcision. For neither circumcision counts for anything nor uncircumcision, but keeping the commandments of God. Every one should remain in the state in which he was called. Were you a slave when called? Never mind. But if you can gain your freedom, avail yourself of the opportunity. For he who was called in the Lord as a slave is a freedman of the Lord. Likewise he who was free when called is a slave of Christ. You were bought with a price; do not become slaves of men. So, brethren, in whatever state each was called, there let him remain with God. (1 Cor. 7:1–24)

127

I have included the whole of this section because the question of wives and fiancées has to be seen within the context of the actual question being asked here.

It seems that one of the problems Paul faced here and elsewhere was the reaction of many Romans and Greeks to their conversion. Paul often used the imagery of freedom from slavery to explain the process of redemption through Christ. Once they were the slaves of sin. Satan was their master and he refused to release them—manumit them. Christ, by his death and resurrection, has freed them—manumitted them—from their ownership by Satan and became himself their master. They are now, like Paul, the slaves of Christ. Redemption, as proclaimed by Paul, was an exchange of ownership, not a freeing from one owner to be a freedman.

Many converts, it appears, inferred that this process of being freed from slavery to Satan also involved the automatic severance from all the contractual relationships that controlled them in their pagan lives. A married man believed that his conversion automatically ended his marriage and he was free of all family responsibilities. If he was an actual slave in bondage to a master, he believed that he was no longer a slave and could simply walk away as though he had become a freedman. This resulted in a great deal of social chaos in Corinth.

Paul's corrective to this problem was to state this important principle: your redemption in Christ changed nothing in your social status and responsibilities. If you were married, then you were to stay married and continue your family duties, but hopefully in a more just and loving way. If you were a slave, then you stayed a slave, but served your master in a way deserving of your new master, Christ.

In looking at women and marriage here, it is important to understand that Paul is dealing with a specific problem and not with generalities. He is dealing with the situation when one partner in a pagan marriage becomes a christian believer. Paul is not addressing the question of deciding whom to marry. Should a wife become a christian believer, then she is not to withhold sex from her husband; nor should the husband if he is the one who is converted. Abstinence from sex is for religious purposes only and is to be decided mutually.

If there is a decision to separate, then it is the non-christian who decides. If the unconverted husband or wife decides to stay in the marriage, then the christian is obliged to agree and continue in the hope that the other partner will eventually become a christian too.

It is important to state here that this passage is not about a christian believer deciding whether or not to marry an unbeliever. Paul deals with that elsewhere. He does suggest that widows and single women who become believers stay single, probably on the grounds that there would not be suitable single believing men available. However, this needs to be tempered with an understanding of the problem that single, unattached women in the ancient world had in trying to survive if they had no male sponsor. One of the reasons that many young widows turned to prostitution was because that was the only work available to them because people were reluctant to employ single women with no family connections. Paul was to have to face that problem later in his letters to Timothy.

The principle of staying in the social level of your pre-christian life also applied to those who had been Jews. They were not to try and surgically undo their circumcision. Those who came to Christ as non-Jews were not to undergo circumcision, since christianity was not a sect of Judaism.

This whole section must be understood in the light of the actual question Paul was being asked, based on the cases of individuals within a marriage who were coming to Christ and whether that fact should automatically end the marriage.

129

We need to remember that marriage was primarily a contract between two families, not a lifelong commitment based upon love. Vows of constancy and permanency are very much a christian concept. Loving and caring for one's partner are also later christian concepts. Paul is here dealing with marriage as he found it in Roman cities. In Corinth, women were very much seen as sex objects and breeders of children. This means that marriage as a christian concept would have been much harder to teach there.

Now concerning the unmarried, I have no command of the Lord, but I give my opinion as one who by the Lord's mercy is trustworthy. I think that in view of the present distress it is well for a person to remain as he is. Are you bound to a wife? Do not seek to be free. Are you free from a wife? Do not seek marriage. But if you marry, you do not sin, and if a girl marries she does not sin. Yet those who marry will have worldly troubles, and I would spare you that. I mean, brethren, the appointed time has grown very short; from now on, let those who have wives live as though they had none, and those who mourn as though they were not mourning, and those who rejoice as though they were not rejoicing, and those who buy as though they had no goods, and those who deal with the world as though they had no dealings with it. For the form of this world is passing away.

I want you to be free from anxieties. The unmarried man is anxious about the affairs of the Lord, how to please the Lord; but the married man is anxious about worldly affairs, how to please his wife, and his interests are divided. And the unmarried woman or girl is anxious about the affairs of the Lord, how to be holy in body and spirit; but the married woman is anxious about worldly affairs, how to please her husband. I say this for your own benefit, not to lay any restraint upon you, but to promote good order and to secure your undivided devotion to the Lord.

If anyone thinks that he is not behaving properly toward his betrothed, if his passions are strong, and it has to be, let him do as he wishes: let them marry—it is no sin. But whoever is firmly established in his heart, being under no necessity but having his desire under control, and has determined this in his heart, to keep her as his betrothed, he will do well. So that he who marries his betrothed does well; and he who refrains from marriage will do better.

A wife is bound to her husband as long as he lives. If the husband dies, she is free to be married to whom she wishes, only in the Lord. But in my judgment she is happier if she remains as she is. And I think that I have the Spirit of God. (1 Cor. 7:25–40)

This is a continuation of the previous passage, but more heavily directed at marriage and betrothal. It should not be assumed that the "present distress" mentioned here is the imminent return of Christ. Paul is writing some eighteen months or so after his first visit to Corinth, in response to some questions he had been sent. He refers earlier to the dissension among the believers there, probably fomented by the false teachers and apostles that had arrived there to undermine his authority.

Also, Paul's two-year residence at Corinth had shown him just how much the Corinthians lived for the moment. "Eat, drink and be merry for tomorrow we die" was very typical of their attitude to life. Everything, like our modern world, was present-driven. Planning and forethought are for philosophers only.

In contrast, Paul indicates that christian believers are future-driven. Forethought is essential to the christian life. People are to marry, not just for the facility of regular sex, but to achieve some future purpose and some solidarity in their lives. This is probably the first time that marriage has been presented as having a purpose outside itself. Marriage is a vocation, a career, and should be treated with the same respect as any other career. This is in marked contrast to the rather cavalier attitudes towards marriage in the Corinth of that day.

For christian women it meant that they were to be treated as human persons with rights and privileges, and not as sexual objects. The marriage bond was to be treated seriously and not broken on a whim. For women, remarriage was to be very carefully thought about, especially since, at this early stage of the development of christianity, there would have been a shortage of unmarried christian men.

The comments about the husband spending so much time and energy pleasing his wife instead of in christian service should be seen within the context of a mixed marriage. So few single christian men and women were at that time eligible that mixed marriage was inevitable. Fathers of unmarried daughters had to maintain their honor and dignity by finding suitable husbands for them. Unmarried men were laughed at, so they, too, needed to find suitable wives.

Where both husband and wife were christians, then the problem of balancing their marriage and their service to Christ is not nearly so critical, for many of the social constraints would have disappeared for them. The expectations associated with pagan preconceptions of rights and duties of husbands to wives, and vice versa, would largely disappear when both partners were christians.

So, Paul's comments should be seen in the light of mixed marriages and not where both partners were christians.

The problem of engaged couples is best understood as a mixed relationship where the husband-to-be is a christian and his fiancée is not. Paul emphasizes the permanency of christian marriage, reminding the man that if he does not think his wife-to-be will be able to come to terms with a christian marriage, he should end the relationship rather than marry to try it out and then face divorce.

Paul is just as concerned here over the woman who, if divorced, will have a most difficult time surviving. It would be better for her if her fiancé broke off the engagement.

> But I want you to understand that the head of every man is
> Christ, the head of a woman is her husband, and the head

> of Christ is God. Any man who prays or prophesies with his head covered dishonors his head, but any woman who prays or prophesies with her head unveiled dishonors her head—it is the same as if her head were shaven. For if a woman will not veil herself, then she should cut off her hair; but if it is disgraceful for a woman to be shorn or shaven, let her wear a veil. For a man ought not to cover his head, since he is the image and glory of God; but woman is the glory of man. (For man was not made from woman, but woman from man. Neither was man created for woman, but woman for man.) That is why a woman ought to have a veil on her head, because of the angels. (Nevertheless, in the Lord woman is not independent of man nor man of woman; for as woman was made from man, so man is now born of woman. And all things are from God.) Judge for yourselves; is it proper for a woman to pray to God with her head uncovered? Does not nature itself teach you that for a man to wear long hair is degrading to him, but if a woman has long hair, it is her pride? For her hair is given to her for a covering. If any one is disposed to be contentious, we recognise no other practice, nor do the churches of God. (1 Cor. 11:3–16)

Sexual identity was extremely important in the Roman world because of the growth of homosexuality and cross-dressing.

This is mirrored in the Old Testament world where marriage, during the wandering in the wilderness, was pretty much an instant affair. A young man came across a young girl in the field and, if she was from a suitable family, he could take her into his tent and make her his wife by having sexual intercourse with her. Imagine his chagrin if he carried her off and then discovered "she" was a man dressed as a woman!

Also, there was a pressing need for Israel to populate as quickly as possible, especially with males as there were wars to be fought. Any practice that prevented acts of sexual intercourse from resulting in pregnancy was proscribed.

But there was also the problem of the way Corinthian prostitutes were dressed so as to be recognisable as prostitutes.

No respectable Roman matron wanted to be propositioned by some drunken sailor!

From studying designs painted on Corinthian pots and created in mosaics, it seems to me that the way the prostitutes did their hair was the main way of displaying their trade. With their hair cut and decorated in outlandish ways, these women immediately attracted the attention of potential customers.

Now think about any of these women who become christian believers. It would take some time for their hair to grow out and look normal. One solution was to shave off the hair and wait for it to grow back normally. But this caused problems, since adulteresses often were forced to have their heads shaved and go bareheaded to atone for the disgrace they brought upon their husbands.

Paul was concerned about those men who wandered around from congregation to congregation. (The word "angel" here need not refer to a heavenly messenger. As sexless beings they are not likely to understand human sexuality, let alone be offended by it.) As they surveyed the women in these small groups, they could easily distinguish those who had once been prostitutes or who had been clean-shaven for adultery. Paul's answer to this problem was to invoke a Jewish custom that required women to wear a veil at worship. If all women wore a veil over their heads, then none of the men could distinguish those who had been prostitutes and those who had not. In a highly sensual society like Corinth, it was important to reduce the sexual undertones of congregational meetings as much as possible. Visiting men wondering about the presence of a prostitute they may well have used would not engender the kind of worshipful attitudes that Paul had in mind!

Again, sexual identity and the social roles that go with it are important to Paul's principle that conversion changes nothing in society generally. Men are not to wear long hair or wear veils. Women are not to wear short hair or remain bareheaded.

Much has been made of Paul's "headship" argument in this passage. What must be continually borne in mind is the general perception that Corinthian men had of their womenfolk. In a society where women were playthings, sex objects and of no status value at all, it was necessary for change to proceed slowly. It would take a generation or two of christianity for women to become respected human beings alongside the men. Paul obviously felt that the best way for christian women to make a mark in the church and in the community was to act appropriately as wives, daughters and mothers. In this way they could build up respect for their sex and engender a whole new basis for their relationships in society.

It is also important to understand that the word "head" is not being used here to mean "chief executive officer." It is being used in its primary meaning as "source" or "coordinator." While the husband is still the focus of the identity and honor of the family, he should not act as though he was the dictator, expecting instant and unquestioning obedience from his wife.

The wife is to play a responsible and responsive part in marriage, not imagining that her conversion has somehow freed her from her marriage contract.

This whole section must be read as a unity and not as separate and separable units.

Within the surrogate family of God that is the church, Paul is stating quite clearly that males and females—the brothers and sisters of their elder brother Christ—are equal in status. The long and involved argument about who was created first and who reflects the glory of God directly, comes down to this one proposition: "Nevertheless, in the Lord woman is not independent of man nor man of woman; for as woman was made from man, so man is now born of woman. And all things are from God" (v.11).

135

Women are to be accorded a dignity and a place in christian society that runs counter to the very low status given them in Corinthian society.

> As in all the churches of the saints, the women should keep silence in the churches. For they are not permitted to speak, but should be subordinate, as even the law says. If there is anything they desire to know, let them ask their husbands at home. For it is shameful for a woman to speak in church. What! Did the word of God originate with you, or are you the only ones it has reached? (1 Cor. 14:33–36)

Here, "in all the churches of the saints" should not be universalized as though all christian congregations around the Roman world and in Jerusalem had this as their rule. You have only to read Paul's letter to the Philippian congregations to understand that this was not the case, for he commends women for their ministry. I have no doubt that Paul was referring to all the gatherings of christian believers in the Roman province of Achaia, an area that covered a great deal more than the capital, Corinth, itself. It must not be imagined that the city of Corinth was the only place in Achaia Paul visited and established congregations. He most probably journeyed to several of the towns and villages in the vicinity, wanting to meet up with the families of those who had come to Corinth for their weekly shopping, heard him and had been converted. He would have wanted to help them set up their own house churches. And, also, at this early stage in their development, christian congregations were not aware of what was happening elsewhere in the world.

We can have no idea at all what actually provoked Paul's outburst against Corinthian women here. All we need to remember is that Paul encouraged the full participation of women in his own missionary work and in congregations outside Corinth. We also need to remember that the only woman deacon named in the New Testament came from Cenchreae, a major seaport of Corinth.

This is not a general prohibition against all christian women to remain silent in church.

In Galatia

The region of Galatia that Paul visited was known as a wild one, even in its day. There were many dialects spoken there, and many races. The ancient Celts were a strong presence there. Paul had come to understand that it was a very multi-cultural area, with Greeks not necessarily being in the major-ity. He had to come to terms with a great number of different religions and philosophies being practiced and taught there.

You have only to read about his experiences in this part of the world to appreciate the problems he must have had with the few christian congregations that arose there (Acts 13 and 14).

His letter to the various congregations scattered around Galatia is a careful statement of the basic christian doctrines, taking note of some of the main heresies that were starting to creep in.

> Now before faith came, we were confined under the law, kept under restraint until faith should be revealed. So that the law was our custodian until Christ came, that we might be justified by faith. But now that faith has come, we are no longer under a custodian; for in Christ Jesus you are all sons of God, through faith. For as many of you as were baptized into Christ have put on Christ. There is neither Jew nor Greek, there is neither slave nor free, there is neither male nor female; for you are all one in Christ Jesus. And if you are Christ's, then you are Abraham's offspring, heirs according to promise. (Gal. 3:23–29)

137

This is a clear enunciation by Paul of the principle that all christians related directly to God through Christ as individu-als and not as constructed by their society. No matter how a society organises the role and status of its tribes, races and sexes, God recognises no differences at all and treats every person as a sibling of Christ.

If the status of males and females in Christ is that of social equals, then that should have brought about a revolution in the place of women in the christian congregations. Sadly, it did not happen, even though Paul, in the way he used women as equal members of his missionary teams, tried to set the standard. But social attitudes passed on from parent to child over many generations do not go away overnight.

For women, Paul's dictum did not mean that they had to become men in order to become "sons of God." (There is a strange passage in the Gospel of Thomas [logion 114] where Jesus talks about Mary Magdalene having to become a man before she can be acceptable.) Nor did it mean that they had to disregard their social roles and responsibilities.

The insistence by Paul in other letters that husbands treat their wives by loving them as themselves was a sure way of breaking down the oppressed situation of women in marriage. But sadly, like the direction to treat slaves as equals, this did not lead to a revolution in women's roles for a thousand or more years. Paul seems intent on preserving the overall social relationships while at the same time challenging christians to adopt different attitudes within those roles.

Sadly, Paul's dictum about all being one in Christ has never to this day been fulfilled to the letter in any christian denomination.

At Ephesus

Ephesus was the virtual capital of Asia and Asia Minor. It had been given a great deal of independence by Rome and was the center of commerce and trade for the whole of the Roman province of Asia.

The worship of Artemis was the key to understanding the

social importance of women in Ephesus. By this time, Ephesus had become the headquarters of the cult of Artemis; the statue and temple there were one of the wonders of the ancient world. Artemis was the guardian of virginity and motherhood. Artemis, twin of Apollo, was a powerful divinity, reflected in the elevation of women socially in Ephesus. What we have here is the opposite of what happened in Corinth, where the worship of Aphrodite resulted in depravity, especially of women.

In Ephesus, men married to enhance their social status. Husbands were noted for the way they lavished their wives with slaves and apparel. The reputation of a husband could be made or broken by the way his wife made her appearances in public.

This aspect of Ephesian life must be kept in mind when reading what Paul has to say about the roles of husbands and wives.

Be subject to one another out of reverence for Christ. Wives, be subject to your husbands, as to the Lord. For the husband is the head of the wife as Christ is the head of the church, his body, and is himself its Savior. As the church is subject to Christ, so let wives also be subject in everything to their husbands. Husbands, love your wives, as Christ loved the church and gave himself up for her, that he might sanctify her, having cleansed her by the washing of water with the word, that he might present the church to himself in splendor, without spot or wrinkle or any such thing, that she might be holy and without blemish. Even so husbands should love their wives as their own bodies. He who loves his wife loves himself. For no man ever hates his own flesh, but nourishes and cherishes it, as Christ does the church, because we are members of his body. "For this reason a man shall leave his father and mother and be joined to his wife, and the two shall become one flesh." This mystery is a profound one, and I am saying that it refers to Christ and the church; however, let each one of you love his wife as himself, and let the wife see that she respects her husband.

139

> 6:1 Children, obey your parents in the Lord, for this is right. "Honor your father and mother" (this is the first commandment with a promise), "that it may be well with you and that you may live long on the earth." Fathers, do not provoke your children to anger, but bring them up in the discipline and instruction of the Lord.
>
> Slaves, be obedient to those who are your earthly masters, with fear and trembling, in singleness of heart, as to Christ; not in the way of eye-service, as men-pleasers, but as servants (slaves) of Christ, doing the will of God from the heart, rendering service with a good will as to the Lord and not to men, knowing that whatever good any one does, he will receive the same again from the Lord, whether he is a slave or free. Masters, do the same to them, and forbear threatening, knowing that he who is both their Master and yours is in heaven, and that there is no partiality with him. (Eph. 5:21–6:9)

Unfortunately in many editions of the New Testament the opening verse, "Be subject to one another out of reverence for Christ," is separated off from what follows by a subheading, leading to a misunderstanding of what Paul is actually teaching.

Christians are to defer to each other in Christ, and this is to be the guiding principle in all their social relationships as christians. Paul then spells out what this means for three sets of relationships: husbands and wives, parents and children, masters and their slaves.

In each case, each partner is to defer to the other. This means that there is no ruling partner with absolute control over the other. There is no partner socially superior to the other by virtue of the marriage. This, in effect, served to break down the oppressive rule of husband over wife, father over children and master over slaves. The social structures remained, but the attitudes of the partners within the structures were completely revolutionized.

How, then, was a wife to defer to a husband while at the same time the husband was to defer to the wife?

In the case of the husband he was to love his wife—be totally committed to her welfare—in the same sacrificial way that Christ loved—was totally committed to—the church. This meant putting her and her needs ahead of his. This was a total reversal of the way husbands generally behaved in Asia Minor at the time. Not only did the husband have absolute right over his wife, but he also married her, as I have already pointed out, in order to advance his own social status. The rich husbands always provided their wives with costly and fashionable clothing and many slaves, but did this in order to advance their own standing in the community. Bystanders would say, "Look how Cornelius dresses his wife—look at all those household slaves that accompany her! Isn't he a great man!" In this way the husband's ego was being fed; it did not mean that he really cared about his wife for her own sake.

I would interpret Paul's words in this way:

> Now look here, you husbands! Now that you are christians you must stop treating your wives as status objects. Up until now you considered only yourselves and the esteem that others gave you because of your wife. But now as a christian husband you must put your wife's personal interests above your own. You must be genuinely committed to her welfare, without a single thought of any kudos you may receive in return. You must be totally committed to her, not to yourself. You must love her sacrificially as Christ loved the church. You must give yourself to your wife and give up all notions of self-interest and status.

Paul's words to these men of Asia Minor would have struck terror into their hearts. Defer to their wives? Look after their welfare for their own sakes?

In return—and this is the key—in return for this self-sacrificing commitment to her, the wife was to obey her husband in the knowledge that what he would ask of her would be no different from what Christ asked of him.

What we have here is almost, but not quite, conditional obedience. The wife's obedience is based upon the husband's commitment to her. What so often happens today is that a man will point to the need for his wife's obedience to him without at the same time acknowledging her right to his self-sacrificing on her behalf. Mutual deference means mutual submission; and this mutuality is based upon the equality of both parties in Christ.

"Headship" here is clearly about source and not structural authority. Christ is the source of the church, having died and been raised to found the church, giving birth to individual believers. So the husband is the founder of the family, being the one who invited his wife to join him in this partnership. He then fathers children in that marriage and is thus the source of that family. And as Christ is the self-sacrificing founder of the church, so is the husband the self-sacrificing founder of his family. There is no question here of the wife being the junior partner in christian marriage.

The same logic then flows on to the relationship between father and children. In that society children had no status at all. The eldest son took over the status of head of the family only at the death of his father. Underaged children had no status or rights at all.

This means that Paul's call for fathers to defer to their children by not provoking them through demanding total and unthinking obedience was a turning upside down of family values. When fathers defer to their children in this way, then children are to defer to their father's will because they will know that what is being asked of them is for their own good. They would be glad to honor such fathers.

Again, family structures have not been interfered with. The family will look like any other family, except that the attitudes of the members to each other will be rather different.

The same process occurs with masters and slaves. Each is

to defer to the other, with the obedience of the slaves being prompted by the caring attitude of the masters. The other important thing here is that Paul does not distinguish between male and female slaves. In the Roman world female slaves were treated very differently from male slaves. For Paul, sex differences do not apply: all slaves are to be treated with respect.

It is important to remember the Asia Minor context in which this letter was written, whether by Paul or by someone writing in his name. No attempt should be made to universalize this material without first taking the context into account and then allowing for the effect of other contexts on the principles that Paul was applying.

> I desire then that in every place the men should pray, lifting holy hands without anger or quarreling; also that women should adorn themselves modestly and sensibly in seemly apparel, not with braided hair or gold or pearls or costly attire but by good deeds, as befits women who profess religion. Let a woman learn in silence with all submissiveness. I permit no woman to teach or to have authority over men; she is to keep silent. For Adam was formed first, then Eve; and Adam was not deceived, but the woman was deceived and became a transgressor. Yet woman will be saved through bearing children, if she continues in faith and love and holiness, with modesty. (1Tim. 2:8–15)

Writing some years later to Timothy who was then in Ephesus looking after the congregations there on his behalf, Paul continued with his concern for women that they do not step outside their structural role in society, while at the same time engendering christian attitudes in their lives.

They were accustomed to dress and decorate their hair in order to add to the status and honor of their husbands. Paul was asking that they dress themselves and have hairstyles that draw attention to that modest way of life that befits the wife

143

of a husband who puts Christ and not himself as the head of his family.

The role of wife in Ephesus, given the social context, is best expressed in child-rearing rather than in being a society showpiece, or in trying to outdo her husband socially by pretending to have authority over him.

Here, as at Corinth, the pagan worship was dominated by a female god; but in this case it was Artemis who was associated not so much with sexual licence as with birth and motherhood.

Paul's interpretation of the Genesis account of the fall is inconsistent with the narrative itself, which makes it quite plain that Adam himself was there with Eve during the temptation by the serpent, and that he acquiesced. What we are to make of this today is a difficult question that I do not think has yet been satisfactorily resolved.

> The women likewise must be serious, no slanderers, but temperate, faithful in all things. (1Tim. 3:11)

Who were these women? Were they female deacons or wives of deacons? The Greek word for "wife" is the same as that for "woman." There is no difficulty with them being women deacons in the light of Phoebe. It is interesting here that women are not being asked to be subordinate to the men. But they are being asked to have the same attitudes as the men.

> Do not rebuke an older man but exhort him as you would a father; treat younger men as brothers, older women as mothers, younger women like sisters, in all purity. (1Tim. 5:1–2)

Bearing in mind that Timothy was not acting as a bishop in Ephesus, but as Paul's temporary representative, it is interesting to note that his structural authority is being tempered with his christianity. In that society, the old men of the tribe were to be respected, but not necessarily obeyed unquestioningly; the older brother did have authority over his younger siblings—male and female—and mothers were respected but secondarily to their husbands.

Paul was demanding of Timothy that he not pretend to a type of apostolic authority that insisted on instant and unquestioning obedience, irrespective of social status. This gives us an important clue to the way Paul himself related to those congregations he founded during his missionary years. Although he claimed to have apostolic authority directly from the Risen Christ, he chose rarely to exercise it in any autocratic fashion.

This does mean that Paul was rather different from the Roman and Greek religious authorities in the way he gave women their due place in the congregations.

Paul's words to Timothy are best understood within the context of the church being a surrogate family, with God as the father and Christ as the elder brother and all human members Christ's siblings and on an equal footing with each other.

Honor widows who are real widows. If a widow has children or grandchildren, let them first learn their religious duty to their own family and make some return to their parents; for this is acceptable in the sight of God. She who is a real widow, and is left all alone, has set her hope on God and continues in supplications and prayers night and day; whereas she who is self-indulgent is dead even while she lives. Command this, so that they may be without reproach. If anyone does not provide for his relatives, and especially for his own family, he has disowned the faith and is worse than an unbeliever.

Let a widow be enrolled if she is not less than sixty years of age, having been the wife of one husband; and she must be well attested for her good deeds, as one who has brought up children, shown hospitality, washed the feet of

> saints, relieved the afflicted, and devoted herself to doing good in every way. But refuse to enrol younger widows; for when they grow wanton against Christ they desire to marry, and so they incur condemnation for having violated their first pledge. Besides that, they learn to be idlers, gadding about from house to house, and not only idlers but gossips and busybodies, saying what they should not. So I would have younger widows marry, bear children, rule their households, and give the enemy no occasion to revile us. For some have already strayed after Satan. If any believing woman has relatives who are widows, let her assist them; let the church not be burdened, so that it may assist those who are real widows. (I Tim. 5:3–16)

The Roman world was rather replete with young widows because so many young husbands lost their lives in wars and skirmishes. The Roman army was the only police force throughout the empire and so it took a great number of men away from the main cities.

The problem widows faced—especially younger ones with no male relatives to look after them—was the restriction they faced in that society to earn money; where younger widows refused to become sex workers, they had little to do with their time, and became a drain on the social work funds of congregations. In these circumstances they congregated in groups and caused trouble, bringing themselves and their congregations into disrepute.

Paul wanted a distinction to be drawn between real widows and those who had some family left to them. It was up to the families of widows to take them back into their homes and look after them, finding suitable husbands where possible. This latter task was difficult when virginity was still valued as the minimum requirement in a prospective wife. But widows with families were not to become dependent on the charity of congregations. Men who refused to look after widows in their own families were acting in a way dishonorable to Christ.

Only those widows with no family to look after them were to have any right to congregational support. This is pared down to widows no younger than 60 years of age who have proved themselves worthy of support by the way they have given themselves to their own families as wives and mothers. Younger widows must marry again and bring up their children in an unblemished christian fashion.

Thus what is really at issue is: "Which husbandless wives are to be defined as 'real widows' and are therefore to be cared for by the congregation?"

Here is what Paul regards as the minimum qualifications for the category of widow worthy of congregational support:

To be over sixty years of age. They would thus be well past childbearing, past sexual promiscuity and too worn-out from family responsibilities to care for themselves.

To have related to only one husband. To have had more than one husband involves the idea of having been committed to more than one man and his extended family, of adapting to the needs of more than one man, or changing loyalties.

To have demonstrated her commitment to her husband by bringing up his children to enhance his reputation.

To have enhanced his reputation for hospitality, especially in serving christians.

To have enhanced his reputation by charitable works, works for the needy, and by doing good in every possible way.

If to us Paul seems rather harsh in his treatment of widows in Ephesus, we must read between the lines and see the extent of the problem there. He saw how undeserved charity was counterproductive. He wanted members of the congregations there to accept full responsibility for their families and help only those widows who were genuinely without family support and who could not contribute to society again by remarrying.

Now, why were widows a problem in Asia, but apparently not elsewhere in the empire?

It was a warring era, so there was a never-ending supply of widows everywhere. But the extended family patterns of that era would have normally met that need. Why not, apparently, in Ephesus?

Bearing in mind the place of women in Ephesus, and that a woman's sole role was to enhance her husband's position, you can see that a "husbandless wife" is a nonperson. Having no husband to live for, a widow has no place in that community. A widow has no value in herself: no status. And that was precisely the problem facing the church. Wives with no husbands could not possibly be accepted as individuals with rights to read the scriptures, pray, prophesy, teach and so on. The general community outside the church would not value a congregation that was composed of nonpersons. The Good News would be brought into disrepute if widows were involved in its work of proclamation.

This is totally in accord with Paul's strategy everywhere he went: he wanted nothing to be said or done that would devalue the Good News in the eyes of the unconverted. It is also quite clear that a prerequisite for consideration as a "real widow" is to have been a perfect wife. Only those who had demonstrated that they had lived blamelessly in the eyes of the general community as the wife of the recently deceased could qualify as real widows and be recipients of the social caring of the congregation.

In no way can verses nine and ten be made to apply to what a husbandless wife had done during her widowhood. She would have to have been a "younger widow" to have achieved all that; and verse fourteen would then apply: she should remarry. Thus a wife unfortunate enough to lose her husband while still young was a wife who had not yet proven herself to be a "good wife." Thus she could not qualify as a real widow.

The only path open for a young widow in Ephesus, therefore, is to marry again and start once more the process of becoming a "good wife." Should she again be widowed she would fail to qualify anyway, since she has now been the wife of more than one husband.

Thus the minimum age of sixty refers to the age at which her husband died, not the age she must reach as a widow before she can qualify for care.

Also notice that in first-century terms, sixty is rather old. A sixty-year-old woman would be physically worn out from all her family duties. Without servants—she needed a husband to keep servants—she would not have been able to care for herself. She would be totally dependent on her family. If she had no family to care for her, then she can claim the charity of her congregation. The idea that at the age of sixty she must qualify for care by enrolling in a religious order of "widows" that will look after other people's children, tend to the clergy and the needy, is monstrous. It is totally out of keeping with the rest of the New Testament and its concerns that we love each other and minister to each other's needs.

A wife who loses her husband at age twenty-five or so is still full of energy. She can care for herself and her children, and earn a living, at least in theory. The problem in Ephesus is that she is now a nonperson: no one will employ her for she has no husband to whom the wages and kudos will go. She then becomes a drifter, her only friends being other younger widows, and a moral danger to all the young men around.

What the writer says in verses 9 to 15 merely reflects what was happening in the community because of the way society regarded young widows.

The sixty-year-old widow is past caring what people think. She is now the object of caring, not a potential carer.

In this whole area the church both accepted the reality of the attitudes of the community around it, and also set a standard of caring where it really mattered.

This passage, then, is about who qualifies for the total caring of the congregation in the matter of one particular category of need: a recently widowed woman over sixty with no close family to care for her in her few remaining years. And notice that these "real widows" are to be honored.

The next problem for Timothy was how to help those young wives at home with not much to do, who were thus at the mercy of wandering teachers and magicians who liked to take advantage of them.

> For among them are those who make their way into households and capture weak women, burdened with sins and swayed by various impulses, who will listen to anybody and can never arrive at a knowledge of the truth. (2 Tim. 3:6–7)

False teachers were a problem very early on in the church, especially in Asia Minor where pagan mystery religions were rife and where there were several philosophers who tried to combine paganism with christianity and created a mixture that horrified Paul.

Young women at home, not very well educated, their husbands away on military service, were especially at risk from these unscrupulous people, who used them for their own purposes, not caring at all for them as individuals. While Paul seems to be denigrating them, he is certainly concerned that they be helped to a better understanding of the faith, as well as playing a more constructively christian part in home and family life.

Timothy will need to treat them as sisters and encourage them back to the true faith.

At Colossae

Wives, be subject to your husbands, as is fitting in the Lord. Husbands, love your wives, and do not be harsh with them. Children, obey your parents in everything, for this pleases the Lord. Fathers, do not provoke your children, lest they become discouraged. Slaves, obey in everything those who are your earthly masters, not with eyeservice, as men-pleasers, but in singleness of heart, fearing the Lord. Whatever your task, work heartily, as serving the Lord and not men, knowing that from the Lord you will receive the inheritance as your reward; you are serving the Lord Christ. For the wrongdoer will be paid back for the wrong he has done, and there is no partiality.

4:1 Masters, treat your slaves justly and fairly, knowing that you also have a Master in heaven. (Col. 3:18–4:1)

This is a condensed version of Paul's household code to the Ephesians. Colossae was also in Asia Minor, and so set in much the same context as Ephesus.

In Crete

But as for you, teach what befits sound doctrine. Bid the older men be temperate, serious, sensible, sound in faith, in love, and in steadfastness. Bid the older women likewise to be reverent in behavior, not to be slanderers or slaves to drink; they are to teach what is good, and so train the young women to love their husbands and children, to be sensible, chaste, domestic, kind, and submissive to their husbands, that the word of God may not be discredited. Likewise urge the younger men to control themselves. Show yourself in all respects a model of good deeds, and in your teaching show integrity, gravity, and sound speech that cannot be censured, so that an opponent may be put to shame, having nothing evil to say of us. Bid slaves to be submissive to their masters and to give satisfaction in every respect; they are not to be refractory, nor to pilfer, but to show entire and true fidelity, so that in everything they may adorn the doctrine of God our Savior.

151

> For the grace of God has appeared for the salvation of all men, training us to renounce irreligion and worldly passions, and to live sober, upright, and godly lives in this world, awaiting our blessed hope, the appearing of the glory of our great God and Savior Jesus Christ, who gave himself for us to redeem us from all iniquity and to purify for himself a people of his own who are zealous for good deeds. (Titus 2:1–14)

Titus is doing in Crete what Timothy was doing in Ephesus: representing Paul, not being a direct supervisor or leader of the congregations there.

This passage is an expansion of the household code as we saw it in both Ephesus and Colossae. There is the same emphasis on preserving the social structures but injecting christian attitudes into them.

In particular Paul is reinforcing the traditional role of the grandmother in the extended Roman family. She was the one who handed on the culture and traditions. She trained the children, especially the females, in the home and family arts and crafts. She inducted them into the mysteries of the married life. Grandmothers also passed on the family traditions to their grandsons, as, for instance, in the case of Timothy, whose grandmother Lois may have been responsible for his initial coming to faith in Christ.

Paul wants all this to continue, but to include christian ways, traditions, attitudes and beliefs.

In summary, then, it can be seen that Paul was more than happy to have women working alongside him in his mission to the gentiles. He invariably names them with a single name and not as the wife of, daughter of, sister of or niece of a family male, as would have been expected in the Roman and Hebrew societies. He is careful to take into account the perceptions of women by the local community so that no taint of scandal can fall upon the reputation of the gospel. He asserts their rights as individuals within family and community structures and is happy for them to have leadership roles when these do not conflict with the social values of the region.

Paul is, nevertheless, still somewhat patriarchal, tending to subordinate women to their menfolk. But it should still be granted to him that he stepped way beyond the mores of his time and continued the process of freeing women to be full members of society, a process begun by Jesus.

153

Others' Comments on Women

Only two other writers in the New Testament make any comments about women and their place in the life of the christian congregations.

Peter

Servants, be submissive to your masters with all respect, not only to the kind and gentle but also to the overbearing. For one is approved if, mindful of God, he endures pain while suffering unjustly. For what credit is it, if when you do wrong and are beaten for it, you take it patiently? But if when you do right and suffer for it you take it patiently, you have God's approval. For to this you have been called, because Christ also suffered for you, leaving you an example, that you should follow in his steps. He committed no sin; no guile was found on his lips. When he was reviled, he did not revile in return; when he suffered, he did not threaten; but he trusted to him who judges justly. He himself bore our sins in his body on the tree, that we might die to sin and live to righteousness. By his wounds you have been healed. For you were straying like sheep, but have now returned to the Shepherd and Guardian of your souls.

Likewise you wives, be submissive to your husbands, so that some, though they do not obey the word, may be won without a word by the behavior of their wives, when they see your reverent and chaste behavior. Let not yours be the outward adorning with braiding of hair, decoration of gold, and wearing of fine clothing, but let it be the hidden person of the heart with the imperishable jewel of a gentle and

> quiet spirit, which in God's sight is very precious. So once
> the holy women who hoped in God used to adorn them-
> selves and were submissive to their husbands, as Sarah
> obeyed Abraham, calling him lord. And you are now her
> children if you do right and let nothing terrify you.
>   Likewise you husbands, live considerately with your
> wives, bestowing honor on the woman as the weaker sex,
> since you are joint heirs of the grace of life, in order that
> your prayers may not be hindered. (1 Pet. 2:18–3:7)

In comparison to Paul, Peter is far more patriarchal and tied to his Hebrew tradition. His version of the household code that Paul uses twice in his letters lays heavier stress on the subordinate and deferential role of women, as well as that of slaves. He has nothing to say to slave masters.

The principle Peter is enunciating is "Be subject for the Lord's sake to every human institution." This is rather different from Paul's principle of mutual deference irrespective of social status.

Peter's letters are far less localized than Paul's, being addressed to christians of Jewish origin among the dispersion "in Pontus, Galatia, Cappadocia, Asia and Bithynia." His target audiences are thus in the eastern half of the Roman empire. Like Paul, Peter is particularly concerned with those wives who became christians while their husbands did not. No doubt he shared Paul's concern that christianity not be charged with an antifamily bias, nor any antigovernment activism.

His Old Testament model of Sarah would hardly appeal to twentieth-century christians! After all, did she not encourage Abraham to take her slave girl, Hagar, and have a son by her, rather than believe that God would work a miracle and cause her to have a son in her old age? In many other ways, Sarah was less than an ideal wife.

The problem with Peter is that he has nothing at all to say to husbands, whereas, as we saw, Paul insists that the husband imitate Christ's self-sacrifice in the way he loves his wife. Peter burdens slaves with that responsibility!

Writer to the Hebrews

> By faith Sarah herself received power to conceive, even when she was past the age, since she considered him faithful who had promised. Therefore from one man, and him as good as dead, were born descendants as many as the stars of heaven and as the innumerable grains of sand by the seashore. (Heb. 11:11–13)

The unknown author of this letter is setting forth examples from the Old Testament of faithful obedience to God. Sarah comes in for mention because she believed that God would do the impossible and cause her to give birth well after her normal years of fertility had passed. This is a strange example, given the Genesis (chapter 18) account of Sarah laughing at the idea that she and her husband were capable of being sexually active at their age, and then encouraging Abraham to take her slave girl to bed to have the promised son. However, our unknown author obviously believed that agreeing to try to conceive at such an advanced age was evidence of Sarah's commitment to God's will.

> By faith the walls of Jericho fell down after they had been encircled for seven days. By faith Rahab the harlot did not perish with those who were disobedient, because she had given friendly welcome to the spies. (Heb. 11:30–31)

157

Rahab certainly stands out as a woman who, in spite of her trade, was prepared to trust in the God of the Jews. She later married Salmon and gave birth to the Boaz who married Ruth, and is mentioned in Matthew's genealogy of Jesus. James also refers to Rahab in his letter, using her as an example where good works prove the existence of faith in God (Jas.2:25).

Neither the writer to the Hebrews nor James says anything about the place of women in the church.

It can be seen, then, that the main defendant of the right of women to take a full and equal part with men in the life and work of the early church was Paul of Tarsus. He is often maligned as a misogynist. But I hope that I have shown that, for his day, Paul was ahead of his culture and his own Jewish upbringing.

But, as I will show, even what Paul achieved was soon to be ripped apart, to such an extent that women disappear almost entirely from the leadership and work of the church.

Women in the Post-Apostolic Era

I want now to mention just a few of the later developments to show how women rapidly become excluded from leadership in the church, except for the formation of the orders of deaconess and widow—a device for keeping women firmly under the control of the male hierarchy.

The Apostolic Fathers

This collection of documents dates from the early second century and consists mostly of letters written by bishops to congregations around the empire. There are thirteen of these letters, mostly rather long ones at that. There are three other longish documents that are either sermons or teachings.

In only one of these—the letter of Ignatius to Smyrna—is there any mention by name of women; they are Gavia and Alce, both personal friends of the author. The only other time women come in for mention is to tell them to be submissive to their husbands!

First Epistle of Clement of Rome to the Corinthians
He reminds the Corinthian christians that,

> . . . your womenfolk were bidden to go about their duties in irreproachable devotion and purity of conscience, showing

> all proper affection to their husbands; they were taught to make obedience the rule of their lives, to manage their households decorously, and to be patterns of discretion in every way. (I:3)

Not content with a reminder of what they had already been taught, he goes on to exhort them to

> . . . set our womenfolk on the road to goodness, by teaching them to be examples of lovable purity, to display real sincerity in their submissiveness, to prove the self-restraint of their tongues by observing silence, and to bestow equal affection, with no favoritism and as becomes holiness, upon all God-fearing persons. (XXI:6–7)

Bishop Clement of Rome is certainly not in the mode of the apostle Paul whom he was pleased to quote when it suited him. Women, for him, and especially Corinthian women, were to be kept right in the background, where they were before early christianity had begun to liberate them.

The Epistle of Ignatius to the Smyrnaeans

At the very end he sends greetings "to the families of my brethren who have wives and children; and to those virgins whom you call widows." It seems rather strange to single out those men who are married. Did this mean that Ignatius believed that christian men should remain single, or that he devalued marriage?

The virgins here were probably single unattached women who had no male sponsors and had remained unmarried and were included among those who were in need of special care and attention, not being able to earn their own living.

He sends special greetings to "Gavia and her family," with prayers that she continue faithful and steadfast in her church and community work. He also greets Alce, "who is specially dear to me." He is to refer to her later in his letter to Polycarp. These are the only mentions of women by name in the Apostolic Fathers.

The Epistle of Ignatius to Polycarp
Polycarp was a bishop at Smyrna and was to become one of the best known of the early christian martyrs.

Polycarp issues some instructions, including the following:

> Tell my sisters to love the Lord, and to content themselves physically and spiritually with their own husbands. (V)

This kind of instruction is not given to husbands.

He sends greetings to the unnamed wife of a local civic official, and again to Alce.

The Epistle of Polycarp to the Philippians
Polycarp, Bishop of Smyrna, on his way to Rome where he was eventually to be martyred, had been asked by the church at Philippi whether anyone could deliver their letter to the christians at Antioch in Syria. They also asked for copies of Ignatius' letters. Polycarp sends this letter as a covering note with copies of Ignatius' letters.

He is very much in the mold of Ignatius when it comes to women.

> After that we can go on to instruct our womenfolk in the traditions of the faith, and in love and purity; teaching them to show fondness and fidelity to their husbands, and a chaste and impartial affection for everyone else, and to bring up their children in the fear of God. Widows are to observe discretion as they practice our Lord's faith; they should make constant intercessions for everyone, and be careful to avoid any talebearing, spiteful tittle-tattle, false allegations, over-eagerness for money, or misconduct of any description.

> They are to recognise that they are an altar of God, who scrutinizes every offering laid on it, and from whom none of their thoughts or intentions—no single one of their heart's secrets—can be hidden. (IV:2–3)
>
> The conduct of our young women, equally (with the young men), must show the unblemished purity of their conscience. (V:3)

Here, again, is that stereotyping of females that Jesus and Paul had avoided. Where once women were allowed to be themselves in their own right, they are now back in their subservient role. They are once more the source of sexual sin and must keep themselves and their conscience absolutely pure. I find it interesting that only women are exhorted to have this inner spiritual and moral purity. This is typical of the Mediterranean model that I outlined at the beginning of this book, where women's role is to have that sense of shame that is used to protect men from losing their honor. Pure women, you see, make sure that men do not sin; impure women result in men who sin. Men are thus the victims of women's sexuality.

It can be seen that, in the Apostolic Fathers as a whole, women are very much an inferior caste and a potential source of promiscuity and factionalism in the church. Only two are mentioned by name and one unnamed, the wife of an official.

The contrast with the apostolic era is obvious and tragic.

It was almost inevitable that, once ordained clergy came into being and authority was centered around a monarchical bishop, lay involvement in the mission and leadership of the church would disappear. But, not only did the work of women disappear—other than in service to the community through prayer and the care of widows—their actual status as wives and single women reverted to what it was in prechristian times.

The Didache

This document was known only by reference to it in several early christian works. It did not come to light until the late nineteenth century, when it was accidentally discovered in the library of the patriarch at Constantinople.

It is known simply as "Didache" which is Greek for "teaching," and claims to be an official collection of basic christian teachings handed on by the twelve apostles.

The first half is a sermon-like feature called "The Two Ways," that is, the way of life and the way of death. It reads like exhortations of a father to his son. The only references to women in this section are as follows:

> abortion is forbidden
> discipline both sons and daughters in the fear of the Lord
> don't shout at male or female domestic slaves.

The second section is a kind of church manual, containing rules for the organisation and worship within the congregation. The whole tenor of this manual is thoroughly masculine. There is absolutely no account taken of the possibility that a prophet or teacher or deacon could be a woman. Women just do not rate a single mention.

Thus, women as leaders and workers disappear almost entirely from the church. The only time they emerge is in a group of documents that are more like romantic novels. It seems that these documents, known as "Apocryphal Acts," could have been written from within communities of sexually inactive women as a protest against the disappearance of female leadership and ministry from the church as a whole.

What did remain were two subordinate orders—deaconesses and widows—set up to keep these women under male control. Their only avenue of service was to help the all-male ministry, and to do some social service.

163

Those other documents that have come down to us from gnostic sources invariably construct women as becoming male.

Eusebius' Ecclesiastical History

Writing in the early fourth century of our era, Bishop Eusebius of Caesarea set out as best he could with the resources available to him a history of the church from the birth of Christ to the reign of Constantine. Many of the documents he refers to have not survived, and so the accuracy of quotations in his history cannot always be checked.

Reading through the early sections where he details the history of the church from the death of the last apostle, you soon discover that no women are mentioned in connection with the work and leadership of the church.

Instead of being a motley collection of house churches with no central leadership structures, the church has become centralized around the bishop of a large city, with the bishop of Rome starting to claim primacy. One of the results of this is that lay leadership and participation in congregational life have virtually disappeared, with women receiving no mention at all.

There is a lengthy quote from a document sent from Gaul, describing the martyrdom of four people: Sanctus, Maturus, Attalus and Blandina. The last one was a woman and the account credits her with being the most noble of them all, encouraging the others to remain firm. But Blandina is the only woman mentioned in this post-apostolic period. Eusebius is interested mainly in the bishops, for the history of the bishops is the history of the church. In many ways he did his history in the same way his Greek and Roman predecessors had done: concentrating on the leaders, as though the people had no history of their own.

Even when dealing with the apostolic period, few, if any, women are mentioned by name, other than Mary, mother of Christ. The difference between Eusebius' account and the New Testament documents is immense when it comes to the naming of women.

What began as a movement that offered dignity and equality to women ended up as an organisation that was almost totally androcentric.

The Apocryphal Writings

At the same time that women disappeared from church life, there emerged a spate of writings that were full of women and their daring deeds. The second and third centuries seemed to spawn these fictional accounts of the life of Christ and the apostles, as well as some religious novels.

One scholar has suggested that the writers of these documents were in fact widows. Why widows? Well, married women would not have had the time to do much writing, and I have no doubt that their husbands would not have allowed them to write in such a triumphalist way about women.

I will now give you a summary of the accounts of some of these women and their outrageous actions. I myself have no doubt that these stories were a kind of backlash against the deliberate exclusion of women from the leadership of the church. As the canonical writings of the New Testament became more widely circulated, women would have been amazed at how important a role women of earlier generations played in their church. Being powerless to correct this, they could easily have found an outlet in writing in the name of some well-known male leader or apostle. They certainly could not write in their own name, for to do so would have been to make sure their work was burned!

The Protevangelion of James

The Virgin Mary must have parents, so two are invented for her: Joachim and Anna. They are under a cloud of shame because Anna is childless. Two angels appear to Anna and promise her a child, who is to be called Mary. The child is offered to the priests at the temple while Anna sings a song reminiscent of the Magnificat of Mary.

When Mary is three years old she is taken to the temple and is educated there while being fed by an angel. At twelve she is miraculously betrothed to Joseph, starts weaving a purple veil for the temple and has an angelic visitation promising her motherhood of the Messiah.

After the birth of Jesus, a woman named Salome, whose hand had withered because she did not believe the midwife's story of the Virgin Mary giving birth, has her hand restored when she goes into the cave where Mary and Jesus are and reaches out to touch the child.

Thus, the whole focus of this story is on Mary and not on either Joseph or Jesus.

Infancy Gospels

A variety of writings claiming to come from either Mary or an apostle began to circulate in the late second century. The following is a summary of the main stories concerning women, most of them to do with Mary.

An old Hebrew woman takes Jesus' foreskin after his circumcision and preserves it in an alabaster box with oil and spikenard—the very box that was used later by the prostitute when she anointed Jesus.

Mary hangs out one of Jesus' swaddling clothes after washing it, a young boy touched it and had his demons exorcised. Mary exorcises a young woman by merely showing her pity. She hands the baby Jesus to a young bride who had been struck dumb by a demon and heals her. She does the same thing for another young woman who is invaded by Satan. This woman then brings some scented water and washes Jesus with it, sprinkles some on a young woman who had leprosy and heals her. A princess who has given birth to a leprous child, on hearing this story, does the same and her son is healed. She brings gifts to Mary in thanks. Many other similar miracles are performed by Mary, using water with which she had bathed Jesus. The rest of this account is replete with miracles performed by Mary.

The Acts of Paul and Thecla

An early church father claimed that The Acts of Paul and Theda was written by an orthodox presbyter of Asia. But the inclusion of a woman, Thecla, who had such a prominent role in this narrative, would be most unlikely, especially from such a legitimate source. Paul is a minor character in this novel.

Here is a summary of her part. Onesiphorus of Iconium invites Paul to preach to the congregation meeting in his house. A virgin named Thecla, whose mother is Theoclea and who is betrothed to Thamyris, is eventually converted by Paul. When Paul is chained in prison as the result of a plot, Thecla bribes her way into the prison and kisses his chains.

Later, Thecla is brought before the governor to explain why she now refuses to marry Thamyris. She says nothing and is condemned to be burned at the stake. She has a vision of Christ and the fires do not touch her because God causes an earthquake and a downpour of rain. She joins Paul as his virgin companion.

Because she refused the advances of Alexander, a magistrate, she is condemned to be thrown to wild beasts. Meanwhile, she is adopted by Trifina, whose daughter had just died. This was to ensure her virginity until she met the wild beasts. Trifina accompanies Thecla to the amphitheatre where the wild beasts are given a chance to lick her feet.

When Thecla is finally stripped naked and thrown among the beasts, they end up bowing down to her. She jumps into the pool of carnivorous fish but they all die. The authorities try every trick to incite a range of wild beasts to attack Thecla, but nothing works. Finally, Trifina dies and the governor calls for Thecla to find out who she really is. Thecla then proclaims her faith in Christ and she is released. Trifina miraculously returns to life and takes Thecla to her home, where many young women are converted to Christ.

Thecla finds Paul and tells him all that has happened to her. She then returns to Iconium to find that Thamyris is now dead but her own mother still living. She is unable to persuade her to become a christian, so she goes off to a mountain retreat and founds a monastic order.

Priests of the cult of Diana hatch a plot to kill her, but she is again saved by a miraculous earthquake. She is translated to heaven at the age of ninety.

There are hardly any points at which this novel touches on anything that happened to the Paul of the New Testament. It seems unlikely that an orthodox presbyter of the second century could have written this for an ordinary congregation. Thecla, and not Paul, is the hero. She acts extraordinarily outrageously and is divinely protected in ways that are not given to men.

Written at a time when women had altogether disappeared from the leadership of the church, it is more likely to have been an attack on the male dominance of the church ministry.

The Acts of John

The central part of this novel is given over to the adventures of one Drusiana, wife of Andronicus. She suffers many things, even death, in her bid to remain true to her faith and her husband. She is resurrected, along with some others, by John.

The point here is that this woman is being set forth as a

true exemplar of the christian faith. No men are so written about in this novel, other than John himself.

Acts of Peter

Simon the magician enters secretly the house of Eubula, a rich woman, and steals her jewels. Peter is told about this and there begins a long and involved story about how the jewels are recovered. Eubula responds by selling all her jewelry and giving the proceeds for the poor, the widows and the orphans, and by committing her heart to the Lord Jesus. She eventually dies in peace.

The mother of a senator pleads for her dead son to be restored to life. Peter raises him up and she gives him 4,000 pieces of gold for the care of widows.

Another rich woman, Chryse, gives Peter 10,000 pieces of gold.

In Rome, Xanthippe, wife of Caesar's friend Albinus, leads a delegation of wives to see Peter, telling him they have left their husbands' beds in order to worship God in sobriety and cleanness.

Once again, it is women who are portrayed as exemplars, not men.

The Acts of Thomas

The ninth act in this novel concentrates on Mygdonia, wife of Charisius, right-hand man of the king Gundaphorus of India.

She hears Thomas and becomes a disciple. This results in her deciding to have no further sexual relations with her husband. He tries everything he knows to persuade her back into his bed, but does not succeed.

Charisius then persuades the king to imprison Thomas after scourging him with 128 blows. But even this does not get him his wife back. She steals some money to try and bribe the prison guards to let Thomas out, but Thomas has already been let out miraculously and meets her. She finally receives baptism.

Still more humiliations await her, but in the process two other women, Tertai and Narcia, are converted.

Thomas is back in prison and now the three women are imprisoned. Thomas is finally martyred. The husbands of Mygdonia and Narcia fail to get them back into their beds and finally leave them in peace to live their lives in chastity.

Apart from Thomas, women are the heroes and exemplars of christian living in this novel.

The Acts of Xanthippe and Polyxena

This fourth-century novel is centered around two prominent women of Spain.

Xanthippe is the wife of Probus, a man of rank, and Polyxena is her sister. She hears about Paul from one of her slaves who had just returned from Rome where Paul was staying. This starts her on a season of prayer to God for enlightenment and for an opportunity to meet this Paul.

Her prayers are answered when Paul arrives in Spain and goes to her city. Probus goes out and finds Paul and brings him to the house. On seeing him, Xanthippe falls down before him and wipes his feet with her hair.

When she asks for baptism from Paul, however, her husband shuts him out of the house and keeps her in her bedroom. But she escapes by bribing a slave, finds Paul in the house of Philotheus and is baptized. She then has a vision of Christ appearing to her. Soon her husband comes in search of her and is also baptized.

Polyxena then wishes to find faith. She has several terrible adventures with demons and wild animals and is finally baptized by Paul, as was her suitor and another man who had sought to carry her off.

This is another novel typical of that period. Its focus is again on women as heroes and exemplars of the true faith.

There are many other instances of female heroes in this apocryphal literature. There can be no doubt that they were written into the narratives to encourage women to be brave and to rise above the invisibility that had been laid over them by the male hierarchy of the church. The writers were careful to portray the apostles as encouraging these women heroes to return to their husbands, so as not to be seen to be devaluing marriage.

But there was an awful dilemma being placed upon married women during this period. On the one hand the ideal christian life was being portrayed as one that included sexual continence. On the other hand, women married to non-christian husbands found it impossible to fulfil this ideal without divorce—a solution not favored by the church.

So we find these novels centering around married women who suffer greatly for the right to remain continent yet stay married to their non-christian husbands.

Thus, outrageousness is being encouraged in women through this fictional literature.

The Apostolic Constitutions

Jump ahead a century or so and the reality of the place of women in the church comes to light. This document is written in the name of "the apostles and elders" and is addressed to "all those who from among the gentiles have believed in the Lord Jesus Christ."

The text is actually from the late fourth century of our era, with many of its "canons" accepted by one or two universal church councils.

The place of women is dealt with in several parts throughout this long document, so I will take them in the order in which they occur.

There is a long diatribe against the "strange and wicked woman" who will lure innocent young men into her bed, taken mainly from the Book of Proverbs. Needless to say, there are no warnings to women about wicked men!

Next "let the wife be obedient to her husband," taken out of 1 Corinthians. This is followed by the account of the virtuous women in Proverbs 31. The good wife is not to over-adorn herself and force other men to take notice of her. You see how men have always been suckers for beautiful women: doesn't it remind you of the argument against women priests and how the poor men in the congregation will have their minds on her body instead of on the Lord?!

Women must not attend the public baths when men are bathing there. They must avoid bathing in the middle of the day but rather go at the tenth hour of the day, and certainly not every day.

They must not be contentious: "It is better to dwell in the wilderness, than with a contentious and angry woman" (Proverbs 21:19). Men, of course, are never contentious!

Widows come under even greater scrutiny than in 1 Timothy. It is clear that an order of widows has been established. Widows under sixty years of age ought not to be admitted, since they may remarry because of their sexual appetite and thus bring dishonor to the order. These younger women should be assisted and supported so that they may not remarry. Second marriages are a breach of the original marriage vows and third marriages are a sign of incontinence, while subsequent marriages are clear indications of fornication and licentiousness. The very young widows should be allowed one subsequent marriage to help them escape foolish lusts. There seems to be nothing said about men remarrying as many times as they wish.

Women are not allowed to teach in the church, only to pray and listen to men teaching. Widows are to stay in their own houses and not visit the houses of other people, especially those of unbelievers.

There follows a long harangue against widows who behave in unseemly ways. Again, I am struck by the fact that no such diatribe is aimed at widowers.

Widows are to accept alms only from the faithful, and be ready to obey the clergy.

Women must not be ordained to the priesthood, as in the pagan religions, and they must not baptize. This is in the context of forbidding the laity generally to do anything that the clergy are ordained to do.

Widows are to pray for those who help them, but women—especially deaconesses—are not to publish abroad their own good deeds.

When a woman is baptized, a deaconess must assist to reduce the physical contact between baptizer and baptized.

Virgins who take a vow of perpetual virginity must behave suitably. Again, no such commands are laid upon men who may take such a vow.

Again, wives are to be subject to their husbands, and husbands are to love their wives as partners in life and fellow helpers in the procreation of children.

In the directions about ordination services, the prayer for the ordination of a deaconess contains the words "cleanse her from all filthiness of flesh and spirit." These or similar words are not used in any services for ordaining men.

"He who has taken a widow, or a divorced woman, or a harlot, or a slave, or one belonging to the theater, cannot be either a bishop, priest or deacon, or indeed any one of the sacerdotal catalog. He who has married two sisters, or his brother's or sister's daughter, cannot be a clergyman."

It can be clearly seen from what I have brought together

from this document that the position of women in the church had greatly deteriorated since apostolic times. The sadness is that a great deal of the attitudes behind such regulations still persists in many sections of the church today.

Conclusion

The evidence from all sources is quite unequivocal: while women of any social status were welcomed and encouraged to take an active part in the life and leadership of the church during the first two generations of christianity, they virtually disappear for the next several generations.

The pattern is so clear as to require no great research. Jesus affirmed women as individuals in their own right without the social necessity to be under the control of a male sponsor. He was honored to have rich women organize the food and accommodation for himself and his male disciples when they journeyed around Galilee. God even chose women to be the first to know of the coming of the Messiah, and to be the first to see and hear the Risen Christ.

Paul was happy to have women work side by side with him in his missionary work around Greece. He is comfortable with women being the head of house groups of worshipping christians. He did have some problems with a few women in places where the outside world constructed women as inferiors and sex objects; but overall he clearly encouraged women to take a full part in the spiritual work of the church.

The only deacon named is a woman, Phoebe.

And then, at the end of the first century of our era, women drop out of sight in the leadership and work of the church. The only exceptions are a very few, very powerful christian women from the ruling classes. Some of these were widowed early in life and were able to use the resources inherited from their husbands to care for widows and orphans.

It seems that there was an excess of elite christian women with no men of similar status to marry. This allowed them to maintain their social status and exert some influence on the church.

But they were not allowed to participate in the ordained ministry, and therefore had no say in policy making. It needs to be remembered that by the turn of the first century, lay participation in church leadership had almost totally disappeared, so there was never any hope for women.

There has been some speculation that there emerged an order of deaconesses, derived from Phoebe, the deacon of Cenchreae. It has even been suggested that the widows of 1 Timothy 5:9 may have been deaconesses. However, in dealing with that passage earlier, I pointed out that the word usually translated "enrolled" really means "considered" and that Paul was defining those who could be categorized as true widows rather than having them enrolled in a list.

Orders of deaconesses and widows did emerge a century or two later, probably in response to the growing numbers of unattached women and the problem of how to manage their care. But these "orders" were firmly under the control of the bishops and were allowed to do only those things that generally men preferred not to do.

The immediate post-apostolic era shows clear evidence of women being put right back into their pre-christian roles.

And then in the wealth of apocryphal literature and historical romances and novels that emerged from the second to the fourth centuries, women are portrayed as heroes and exemplars. There is good reason to believe that such literature was brought into being by rich and powerful women who may have endowed male writers to create these romances and novels as a protest against the disappearance of women from the history of the church.

From then on, to the time of the protestant reformation and the catholic counterreformation, women continue in their inferior and submissive roles.

Just as the growth of the lay ministry among the mainline churches is only a hundred or so years old, so the movement for the recognition of the ministry of women is only relatively recent, outside of religious orders. Even in those denominations that have allowed for ordained women to take part in the life and leadership of the church, they are still placed in roles subservient to the male clergy. In the Salvation Army, for example, while women have been allowed and even encouraged to become officers, they must reduce their rank to that of their husband, and no woman can ever be head of the Salvation Army if she is married to an officer.

I believe that Holy Spirit is awakening and empowering women in all the churches to arise and re-establish their place in the church.

If this means being somewhat outrageous, then recall all those women in the gospels and the early church who defied convention, knowing that God was even more outrageous than they in concentrating on the poor and the powerless, offering them full and equal membership in the kingdom of God, even if that meant defying a whole range of human social conventions.

Indeed, these are exciting times.

Appendix

References in the New Testament (NT), Apostolic Fathers, and New Testament Apocrypha

Adulteress
NT
   Jn. 8:3–11

Anna
NT
   Lk. 2:36–38

Apphia
NT
   Philem. 2

Bernice
NT
   Acts 25:13

Chloe
NT
   1 Cor. 1:11

Claudia
NT
   2 Tim. 4:21

Crippled Woman
NT
   Lk. 13:10–17

Damaris
NT
   Acts 17:34

Drusilla
NT
   Acts 24:24

Elizabeth
NT
   Lk. 1:5, 7, 13, 24, 36, 40, 41, 57
NT Apocrypha
   Gospel of the Ebionites, 3
   Protevangelium of James, 12. 2–3;
     21.3
   Pistis Sophia, c.7
   Life of John According to
   Serapion, 414–15
   (Hennecke, Schneemelcher *et al.*)

Euodia and Syntyche
NT
   Phil. 4:2

Herodias and Daughter Salome
NT
   Mat. 14:3, 6
   Mk. 6:17, 19, 22
   Lk. 8:19

Indigent Widow
NT
   Mk. 12:41–44
   Lk. 21:1–4

Further Reading

The Social Background

Esler, P F, *The First Christians in the Social Worlds:* social-scientific approaches to New Testament interpretation, Routledge 1994

Judge, E A, *The Social Pattern of Christian Groups in the First Century*, Tyndale Press 1960

Leming, M R, DeVries, R G, and Furnish, B F J eds, *The Sociological Perspective*: a value-committed introduction, Zondervan 1989

Malina, B J, *The New Testament World*: insights from cultural anthropology, SCM 1981

Pilch, J J and Malina, B J eds, *Biblical Social Values and Their Meaning*: a handbook, Hendrickson 1993

Theissen, G, *The First Followers of Jesus*: a sociological analysis of the earliest Christianity, SCM 1978

—*The Social Setting of Pauline Christianity*, T & T Clark 1982

The Place of Women

Davies, S L, *The Revolt of the Widows*: the social world of the Apocryphal Acts, SIUP 1980

Dixon, S, *The Roman Mother,* Routledge 1990

Fiorenza, E S, *In Memory of Her,* a feminist theological reconstruction of Christian origins, SCM 1983

Fox, R L, *Pagans and Christians*, Penguin 1986

Heine, S, *Women and Early Christianity*: are the feminists scholars right? SCM 1987

Laffey, A L, *Wives, Harlots and Concubines*: the Old Testament in feminist perspective, Fortress Press 1988

Lefkowitz, M R and Fant, M B eds, *Women's Life in Greece and Rome*: a source book in translation, Duckworth 1982

Pomeroy, S B, *Goddesses, Whores, Wives, and Slaves*: women in classical antiquity, Pimlico 1975

Ryrie, C C, *The Role of Women in the Church*, Moody Press 1958

Stagg, E and F, *Woman in the World of Jesus*, Saint Andrew Press 1978

Witherington III, B *Women in the Ministry of Jesus*, CUP 1984

—*Women and the Genesis of Christianity* CUP 1990

General Reference

Eusebius, *The History of the Church* trans. Williamson, G A, Penguin 1965

Freyne, S, *The World of the New Testament*, Veritas Publications 1980

Hennecke, E, Schneemelcher, W and Wilson, R McL eds, *New Testament Apocrypha*, Westminster Press 1963

James, M R, *The Apocryphal New Testament*, Clarendon 1924

The Apostolic Constitutions in *The Ante-Nicene Fathers Vol. VII*, T & T Clark 1994

Jeremias, J, *Jerusalem in the Time of Christ*, SCM 1969

Malina, B J and Rohrbaugh, R L, *Social-Science Commentary on the Synoptic Gospels*, Fortress Press 1992

Marshall, I H, *Acts*: an introduction and commentary, Tyndale 1980

Staniforth, M and Louth, A eds, *Early Christian Writings*: The Apostolic Fathers, Penguin 1969